# End-of-life care
## Promoting comfort, choice and well-being for older people

Jane Seymour, Ros Witherspoon, Merryn Gott, Helen Ross and Sheila Payne with Tom Owen

First published in Great Britain in May 2005 by The Policy Press
in association with Help the Aged

The Policy Press
University of Bristol
Fourth Floor, Beacon House
Queen's Road
Bristol BS8 1QU
UK

Tel no +44 (0)117 331 4054
Fax no +44 (0)117 331 4093
E-mail tpp-info@bristol.ac.uk
www.policypress.org.uk

ISBN 1 86134 761 8

British Library Cataloguing in Publication Data
A catalogue record for this report is available from the British Library.

Library of Congress Cataloging-in-Publication Data
A catalog record for this report has been requested.

Cover design by Qube Design Associates, Bristol
*Front cover:* photograph by Nigel Cockrell
Printed in Great Britain by Latimer Trend, Plymouth

# Contents

# Preface

I am pleased to introduce this groundbreaking research report on end-of-life care, commissioned by Help the Aged and carried out by Jane Seymour and colleagues at the University of Sheffield. The research was undertaken by Help the Aged in response to our key strategic aims: to defeat ageism, challenge poor standards and promote quality in care. By publishing and disseminating this report, we hope that we can improve the experience of older people at this final stage of life.

This report provides a comprehensive account of the available evidence on the circumstances and needs of older people who are dying within the UK. It paints a picture of how and where older people die, the services that they receive and how older people communicate with regard to end-of-life issues. It also critically examines the policy context underlying end-of-life care for older people and provides recommendations for practice and research. This is the first time that research findings on this theme have been pulled together and presented in one report.

An alarming conclusion of the research relates to the huge inequality that older people experience in terms of the care and support they receive at the end of life despite the often highly complex multiple health conditions affecting them. The evidence clearly demonstrates that older people who are dying are less likely to be admitted to a hospice compared with younger people in similar circumstances. Older people are less likely to die in their place of preference, are more likely to experience repeated hospital admissions and are less likely to receive proper preventative planning as they near the end of life compared with younger people. Moreover, older people are often not fully involved in discussions concerning the options available to them at the end of life, without which appropriate choices and decisions cannot be made to meet the individual's needs.

It is clear that urgent measures are required to address the age discrimination that exists in relation to services for the dying. Many older people do not have access to support services that are sufficiently flexible to meet their physical, emotional and social care needs at the end of life. In improving such services, a guiding principle must be that older people are properly engaged in their development.

This report is a result of much hard work and we thank Jane Seymour and her colleagues for their considerable efforts. The report feeds into an increasing amount of policy and service development work in relation to end-of-life issues that is being undertaken by Help the Aged. This report demonstrates that considerable work remains to be done in helping to minimise the distress and maximise dignity for older people at the end of their lives.

*Michael Lake CBE*
*Director General, Help the Aged*

# Acknowledgements

The project was assisted greatly by Tom Owen and his colleagues at Help the Aged, and by attendees at a consultation meeting held in Sheffield on 9 June 2004, where key themes in the report were presented and discussed with a group of older adults and voluntary group representatives. Tom Owen invited a number of older people to author short articles about their views and experiences relating to these issues. We are very grateful for the time, care and thoughtfulness that the contributors devoted to their writing. The results are both moving and insightful, giving a valuable and deeply personal view of how the issues addressed in this report are encountered in daily life.

# Executive summary

This report is the result of a comprehensive review of evidence regarding the circumstances, experiences and preferences of older people in relation to end-of-life care. In particular, we draw upon this evidence to suggest policy and practical recommendations for the improved care and support in the UK of older people who are approaching death and their carers.

The report is divided into five chapters:

## Chapter 1: Definitions, policies and practices: the broader context of end-of-life care

- Provides an overview of the picture of mortality in the UK, including causes of death.
- Explains key terms, including end-of-life care, palliative care, terminal care, continuing care and supportive care.
- Discusses the relationship between palliative and geriatric care.
- Examines key policy issues that affect end-of-life care for older people.

## Chapter 2: Patterns, circumstances and experiences of end-of-life care among older people

- Focuses on changes in the demography of ageing, drawing out the implications of these for health and illness in older age.
- Explores the concepts of comorbidity and frailty in later life.
- Examines the importance of carer availability in enabling older people to live (and die) at home.

- Looks at the end-of-life experiences of older people with heart failure, dementia and those in late old age.

## Chapter 3: 'Places' of care at the end of life

- Examines settings of care for older people at the end of life.
- Explores older people's preferences for place of care at the end of life.
- Draws comparisons between the experiences of older people who receive specialist palliative care and those who do not.

## Chapter 4: Communication and decision making at the end of life

- Examines whether older people welcome opportunities to discuss death and dying.
- Explores decision making at the end of life, particularly in relation to 'advance care planning', consent and autonomy.

## Chapter 5: Conclusion and recommendations

- Draws together some conclusions and makes a range of recommendations for practice, policy and research.

# Introduction

*Jack died in the end of a lung infection. But what in fact killed him was a combination of Parkinson's disease, severe arthritis, enlarged prostate and a damaged heart. During the year and a half of his final illness, he was treated by three sets of specialists for these different ailments and was shunted back and forth between three different hospitals as each in turn was attended to. As a result his notes were frequently lost or delayed or sent to the wrong hospital; he often spent days, even weeks, without being treated at all, while the hospital he was in worked out what to do with him; and most serious of all, he invariably lost out on the care of the ailments that weren't that particular hospital's speciality.... The problem was that while there were lots of people in charge of different parts of Jack's body, none was in charge of Jack.... All of us in the family suspected that Jack was dying from the moment he first contracted his first bladder infection to the day he finally did die a year and a half later.... The fiction that, apart from Parkinson's, his problems were temporary and that he would stride out of hospital to resume a reasonably normal life was maintained until the end. It was fiction that deprived Jack of the care he really needed.* (Hoyland, 1997, p 8)

Today, 83.5% of deaths occur among people aged over 65[1], and this is likely to rise over the next three decades as the postwar 'baby boomers' enter their eighties. Many older people remain in good health well into late old age. However for some, ageing brings with it the experience of chronic life-limiting illness, reduced resources to retain independence and

fundamental inequalities in health and social care provision. For these older adults, the last months and years of life involve 'living on thin ice' (Lynn and Adamson, 2003), with general, non-specific deterioration in health and quality of life interspersed with periods of acute illness. They face repeated hospital admissions, under-recognition of symptoms, lack of preventive planning and inadequate home support. There is little or no knowledge of older people's perceptions about this stage of their life or their practical, social, spiritual and existential concerns. Moreover, it is unclear from where or from whom they would prefer to seek information or help to address these concerns, or indeed, whether instead they perceive these matters as entirely private.

It is paradoxical that in the face of this gap in our knowledge a consensus has been widely established that, ideally, we should all be able to expect a death where there is privacy, dignity, good-quality care in comfortable surroundings, adequate pain relief and appropriate support in keeping with our preferences (General Medical Council, 2002). This model of 'good death' was spearheaded in part by the development of the modern hospice movement founded in 1967 by Dame Cicely Saunders at St Christopher's Hospice in London (Saunders and Baines, 1983). Saunders' mission was to convince others that dying people should not be deserted in the time of their greatest need, but should be cared for in a manner that enables them to live as fully as possible, and is respectful both of their wishes and of their uniqueness as persons. Talking about and planning how one wants to live the last stages of life is an important aspect of achieving this (Help the Aged, 2002).

This report is the result of an enquiry into what has been written about the circumstances, experiences and preferences of older people in

---

[1] www.statistics.gov.uk/StatBase/Expodata/ Spreadsheets/D8257/xls (accessed 15 June 2004).

relation to end-of-life care. Our intention has been to draw on evidence of these to suggest policy and practical recommendations for the improved care and support in the UK of older people who are approaching death and their carers.

The objectives of the report are:

- To outline the current policy and practice context within which health and social care to dying people is delivered and to indicate areas of key relevance to older people and their carers.
- To identify the range of patterns and circumstances of death and dying[2] encountered in older age.
- To examine issues resulting from a comparison of dying older people who receive specialist palliative care in the last year of their lives and those who do not.
- To explore key issues in older people's experiential accounts of death, dying and bereavement, with special reference to decision making concerning place of care and processes of care.
- To describe factors that older people identify as important in achieving good standards of care at the end of life[3].

---

2   'Dying' is difficult to identify prospectively. It will therefore be defined as the last year of life.

3   The term 'good standards of care at the end of life' will be defined using the perspectives of older people, but also in terms of the recent guidance from the General Medical Council (2002) in which it is stated that: "Patients who are dying should be afforded the same respect and standard of care as all other patients. Patients and their families and others close to them should be treated with understanding and compassion. Where the likely progression of a patient's condition is known, and their death is seen as an inevitable outcome, it is important to ensure that the patient's palliative care or terminal care needs are identified and met appropriately. This should include consideration of their wishes regarding such matters as the appropriate place for receiving care (which may affect the treatment options available), and their needs for religious, spiritual or other personal support. Every attempt should be made to ensure that they are afforded privacy, dignity, and good quality care in comfortable surroundings. This includes assessment of, and adequate relief from, pain and other distressing symptoms, and appropriate support and nursing care" (para 26, available at www.gmc-uk.org/standards).

- To identify what informal or formal opportunities exist for older people and their carers to discuss and obtain reliable information about social, spiritual and care issues related to death, dying and bereavement, and to make a preliminary exploration of preferences associated with these.

## Parameters of the study

The project has involved three key activities: a literature review; a secondary analysis of data and a consultation exercise.

### The literature review

A wide range of literature has been reviewed, focusing mainly on sources of relevance that have been published in the last decade. Most of the material reviewed is from the UK, although we make some reference to the international literature where it has been helpful to do so. Occasional reference is made to earlier work, where it is of seminal importance or demonstrates a particular trend well.

We have examined the policy- and research-based literature as it relates to palliative and end-of-life care, ageing, chronic illness and informal caring. Selectivity, using our professional judgment, has been necessary to cover such a broad field. We have taken the advice of colleagues where possible and have tried to include only those sources that are specifically relevant to the situation of older people facing the end of their lives and to our stated objectives. We have examined sources in the social science, gerontology, nursing, medical and specialist palliative care fields, with a particular emphasis on gaining understanding of the links between comorbidity, 'frailty', late old age and experiences of end-of-life care, death, dying and bereavement. In examining the policy literature relating to older age, we were struck by a general lack of reference to end-of-life care; this seems largely to have been left to the pursuit of the specialist palliative care organisations, which of course have a much wider remit than older adults. As a consequence, the needs of older adults facing death have been neglected.

The report was prepared at a time of increased interest in issues of palliative and end-of-life care. There has been a Health Committee Inquiry into Palliative Care during 2004[4], comprehensive guidance on supportive and palliative care for adults with cancer was published in the same year and a review of legislation regarding mental capacity and assisted dying is under way. It is hoped that this report will help to inform these important debates.

## Secondary data analysis

Between 2001 and 2003 a team at the University of Sheffield carried out a study funded by the Economic and Social Research Council (award reference: L218252047). This used an innovative methodology developed in partnership with community groups to explore the views of older people about end-of-life care. Pictures, story boards and media extracts were used to address issues in interviews and focus groups, and the research team was assisted by an advisory group that included participants. Seventy-seven older people from three age cohorts (65-74; 75-84; 85 years and over) and from three contrasting areas of Sheffield took part, some of whom attended a one-day dissemination and discussion meeting in March 2003. This report includes some targeted secondary analysis of data from the study and also draws on recent publications relating to the study (Seymour et al, 2002b, 2003, 2004).

## Consultation exercise

On 9 June 2004, a consultation meeting relating to this project was hosted by Help the Aged and the authors of the report at the Quaker Meeting House in Sheffield. Invitation was made by placing adverts in local newsletters and by utilising existing networks. This involved a presentation of a summary of key issues in the report, and lively small-group discussions about the range of recommendations that should be made. A range of people, numbering 22, took part, the majority of whom were older adults and all of whom had a direct interest in the

---

[4] www.parliament.the-stationeryoffice.co.uk/pa/cm200304/cmselect/cmhealth/454/454.pdf (accessed 12 July 2004).

subject matter. Some were older adults who had been bereaved following a period of care giving; some were in the throes of trying to come to terms with the entry of their partner or parent to a care home. Others were representatives of community groups for older adults. One person, who was unable to attend the meeting because of his health, was visited at home to enable his contribution to the consultation. Participants included representatives from the African Caribbean community, the Chinese community and the Asian community.

## Structure of the report

The report is in five chapters:

- Chapter 1 provides some definitions, and reviews the policy context within which older people in the UK face death.
- Chapter 2 reviews how and where older people die, drawing attention in some detail to issues facing older people who die of heart failure or dementia, or in late old age.
- Chapter 3 explores where older people die and provides some examples of initiatives to improve the care of the dying in all settings of care.
- Chapter 4 explores older people's views on talking about end-of-life care, their views about the 'good death' and their experiences relating to end-of-life decision making. Here, we look critically at the notion of 'autonomy' and outline some key issues relating to consent and advance care planning.
- Chapter 5 sets out recommendations for policy, practice and research.

Seven short narratives have been written by older people (Appendix A) as part of the programme of work on death and dying that Help the Aged is undertaking. The writers were approached by Tom Owen, Research Manager for Help the Aged, and have been supported to express their own voice on end-of-life issues. The articles are included within this report as supplementary information to the research review. The opinions of the writers are not necessarily those of Help the Aged or of the older population as a whole. The articles do, however, offer the reader a real insight into some of the issues and concerns that older people have around death and dying.

# Definitions, policies and practices: the broader context of end-of-life care

## Mortality in the UK: the general picture

In 2001, 580,596 people died of natural causes[1]. The major recorded primary causes of death among all ages are:

- circulatory diseases (41%);
- cancer (27%);
- respiratory diseases (13%);
- mental and behavioural disorders, including vascular dementia (3%);
- diseases of the digestive system (5%);
- Alzheimer's disease and senility (3%);
- genito-urinary diseases (1.5%);
- musculoskeletal diseases (0.9%).

While some adults die suddenly, perhaps with a pre-existing condition that has not caused them much distress, many others experience months of suffering prior to death. Adults with advanced cancer or organ failure (whether as a result of a neurological condition, heart failure or chronic lung disease), and those with extreme general frailty or a number of coexisting conditions (such as dementia and osteoarthritis) (Joy and Standford, 2004, p 6) fall into this category.

People who die from chronic, degenerative diseases other than cancer tend to be aged over 65 years and to have a prolonged illness trajectory that culminates, in the majority of cases, in death within the confines of the acute hospital[2]. In the UK, evidence has been accumulating since the early 1970s that suggests that the experience of dying and death for this group of people and their carers is marked by extreme disadvantage in terms of health and social care provision, particularly specialist palliative care (Grande et al, 1998). We examine the circumstances and patterns of death among older people in more depth in Chapter 2.

*Within a population of 1,000,000 there are approximately 2,800 cancer deaths per year and of these 2,400 people will experience pain, 1,300 will have trouble with breathing, and 1,400 will have symptoms and nausea in the last year of life. There will be approximately 6,900 deaths due to progressive non-malignant disease and some of these will have had a period of advancing progressive disease when palliative care would have been appropriate. Four thousand, six hundred people will have suffered pain, 3,400 will have had trouble with breathing and 1,900 will have had symptoms of vomiting or nausea in the last year of life.* (Higginson, 1997, p 1)

Of course, the degree of suffering endured before death is not only determined by physical illness: deprivation and disadvantage compound suffering. For example, every winter in the UK between 20,000 and 50,000 vulnerable older people die from cold-related illnesses, which exacerbate co-existing chronic conditions.

---

[1] Section 9.5, www.statistics.gov.uk/downloads/theme_compendia/Aa2003/AnnualAbstract_2003.pdf (accessed 5 May 2004). The distinction is made between 'natural causes' and 'external causes', with the latter including accidents, falls, poisoning, self-harm and suicide, homicide and assault, and undetermined intent.

[2] Table 17: Deaths, place of occurrence, www.statistics.gov.uk/downloads/theme_health/DHI_34_2001.pdf (accessed 17 June 2004).

These figures are the 'tip of the iceberg' in relation to the burdens of fuel poverty, cold and damp housing, and social isolation that many vulnerable and ill older people carry. All of these are key factors contributing to suffering in the last years and months of life (Wilkinson et al, 2001; Help the Aged, 2003).

## Key terms

In this report, we have used a working definition of the last year of life to mean the 'end of life', but clearly this can only be established retrospectively. Other key terms we used have been defined as follows.

### End-of-life care

'End-of-life care' is a broad term that encompasses more than the phase immediately before death. The term originates from North America, where it has been used particularly in the context of the care of older people.

> *End-of-life care for seniors requires an active, compassionate approach that treats, comforts and supports older individuals who are living with, or dying from, progressive or chronic life-threatening conditions. Such care is sensitive to personal, cultural and spiritual values, beliefs and practices and encompasses support for families and friends up to and including the period of bereavement.* (Ross and Fisher, 2000, p 9)

Caution needs to be exercised in use of the term end-of-life care. In Australia, this is currently equated with the last few days of life. In the UK, the term 'end-of-life care' has been used by the Department of Health (DH, 2001) without a clear definition being given.

In thinking about end-of-life care, certain terms have been used commonly in the UK policy and practice literature, sometimes rather loosely. Here we give accepted definitions of those terms, and highlight some problems with their use.

### Palliative care

The World Health Organization (WHO)[3] describes palliative care as an approach that improves the quality of life of individuals and their families facing the problems associated with life-threatening illness, through the prevention and relief of suffering by means of early identification and impeccable assessment and treatment of pain and other problems, physical, psychosocial and spiritual. Palliative care:

- provides relief from pain and other distressing symptoms;
- affirms life and regards dying as a normal process;
- intends neither to hasten nor postpone death;
- integrates the psychological and spiritual aspects of patient care;
- offers a support system to help patients live as actively as possible until death;
- offers a support system to help the family cope during the patient's illness and in their own bereavement;
- uses a team approach to address the needs of patients and their families, including bereavement counselling, if indicated;
- enhances quality of life, and may also positively influence the course of illness;
- is applicable early in the course of illness, in conjunction with other therapies that are intended to prolong life, such as chemotherapy or radiation therapy, and includes those investigations needed to better understand and manage distressing clinical complications.

The WHO has adopted an explicitly public health orientation to the promotion of palliative care, and has been concerned to distance this definition from the close association with cancer that characterised an earlier definition. It thus promotes a broad vision of palliative care that is relevant to all those with chronic illness and their families, with the intention of informing policy decisions about minimum standards for comprehensive palliative care for all in need (Sepulveda et al, 2002). Appendix E sets out key policy developments in palliative and supportive care.

[3] www.who.int/cancer/palliative/definition/en (accessed 6 May 2004).

## The provision of palliative care

Clearly, patients' families and other carers are often the most important source of day-to-day care for people with palliative care needs. The professionals involved in providing palliative care fall into two categories:

- those providing general care to patients and their family carers, for example the GP or district nurse;
- those who specialise in palliative care (consultants in palliative medicine, or clinical nurse specialists in palliative care – some of these may be called Macmillan nurses). Specialist palliative care is necessary for people who have unresolved symptoms or complex psychosocial issues, complex end-of-life issues, or complex bereavement issues (NICE, 2004, para 116, p 21). It can be delivered in hospices, hospitals, at home or in care homes.

Currently, specialised palliative care tends to be provided mainly to people with advanced cancer, and its provision is uneven around the country (NCHSPCS, 1999). There is evidence that those who die of non-malignant diseases have as many complex care needs (thus potentially requiring specialist palliative care provision) as those with advanced cancer (Addington-Hall, 1998). In England, palliative care has been tied even more tightly to cancer in recent years with the establishment of supportive and palliative care networks for people with cancer, paralleling the establishment of cancer networks in the wake of recommendations in the NHS Cancer Plan (DH, 2000a). The networks operate in collaboration with a range of statutory and voluntary sector bodies.

Historically, the voluntary sector has been closely involved with both developing and delivering palliative care services to people with cancer and their carers (Joy and Standford, 2004). This continues to be the case, with charities such as Macmillan Cancer Relief, Marie Curie Cancer Care and Cancer BACUP among many others providing a range of information and direct care services. These organisations also lead campaigns to improve care provision. Volunteers are an important part of the hospice workforce. There are far fewer voluntary sector

organisations that provide care services directly to people with non-malignant disease, although Sue Ryder Care and some of the HIV and AIDS charities are notable examples.

*Hospices and palliative care services in this country, largely developed by charities, are among the best in the world. But as with treatment services, the provision of supportive and palliative care services is uneven across the country. It has not been given the priority it deserves by the NHS. (DH, 2000a)*

## Terminal care

Terminal care is part of palliative care, and usually refers to the management of patients during the last few days or weeks or months of life from a point at which it becomes clear that the patient is in a progressive state of decline (NCHSPCS, 1995). The term was used in the 1980s, but has gone out of vogue with the trend towards viewing palliative care as a process and philosophy of care that is applicable from diagnosis until death and into bereavement. We include it here since it is still widely used and understood by professionals and the public. However, the guidance published during 2004 on improving supportive and palliative care for adults with cancer (NICE, 2004, para 114, p 20) warns that the association of palliative care with dying that this term tends to encourage, has negative implications for access and acceptability of palliative care services to those in need. A survey of Health Improvement Plans in England for 1999-2003 (Seymour et al, 2002a) conducted to assess the intentions of health authorities with regard to palliative care found that some thought that palliative care meant just 'care of the dying' or terminal care. This impeded any strategic thinking about the links between plans for palliative care provision and plans for health and social 'continuing' care for people with complex needs and life-limiting illnesses.

## Supportive care

Supportive care is a term that has been introduced in the context of curative cancer care, and underpins recent policy initiatives in this field. It is an umbrella term for all services that can help people with cancer and their families in coping with cancer and its treatment – from pre-diagnosis, through the process of diagnosis and treatment, to cure, continuing illness or death and into bereavement (NCHSPCS, 2002). The key elements of supportive care have been derived from evidence about what people with cancer prioritise, namely, being treated with humanity, dignity and respect; good communication; clear information; symptom control; and psychological support. Box 1.1 summarises government recommendations published in 2004 for improving the supportive and palliative care for

---

**Box 1.1: Guidance on improving supportive and palliative care for adults with cancer: the National Institute for Clinical Excellence for supportive and palliative care**

The guidance defines service models likely to ensure that patients with cancer and their families and carers receive support and care to help them cope with cancer and its treatment at all stages. Although focused solely on services for adult patients with cancer and their families, the recommendations may inform the development of service models for other groups of patients. In a summary of the guidance produced for patients, families and carers by Macmillan Cancer Relief (Macmillan CancerLine 0808 808 2020, or www.macmillan.org.uk/showdocumen t.asp?id=385), the following headings are included:

- You can be involved in decisions about your care
- You can expect your healthcare team to communicate clearly with you
- Your social and practical needs are important
- Your emotional and spiritual needs are also important
  Your family and other carers are important too
- Your preferences about where and how you die should be respected
- You can be involved in making cancer services better. (NCHSPCS, 2004)

---

adults with cancer (NICE, 2004). These clearly have much relevance for adults with diseases other than cancer.

## Continuing care

Also known as 'long-term care', continuing care is "the provision of care over an extended period of time as the result of disability, accident or illness, to meet both physical and mental health needs. It can be provided in a range of settings, from an NHS hospital, care home or hospice, to a person's own home" (DH, 2003, p 97). This type of care is not just concerned with the care of care for older people, but is often used in the context of care for older people. Continuing care may incorporate both health and social care and can be funded out of NHS and social care budgets. Palliative care is one of the various services arranged and funded as continuing care, and is frequently provided in a care home. One major problem here is that funding for specialist palliative care provision is frequently only provided for people with a prognosis of less than six months. This excludes many people in need, and is arguably contrary to the spirit of the recommendations from the WHO and from the National Institute for Clinical Excellence.

## Bereavement and loss

Bereavement usually refers to the period following the death of someone close or someone respected. There are often feelings of grief and desolation. These feelings can also be associated with other types of loss, for example, retirement and the loss of meaningful employment, and loss of the family home. These losses tend to increase as one gets older and it is not uncommon for older people to be coping with multiple losses at the same time. For example, the loss of a lifetime partner who was a carer can result in the remaining partner going into a care home with the consequent loss of the family home and many valued possessions. Much of the bereavement literature is focused on younger death and it is only recently that interest has arisen in the experiences of older people losing lifetime partners (Anderson and Dimond, 1995; Costello and Kendrick, 2000). In Chapter 4, we look in more detail at this literature and the questions it raises about our current understanding of bereavement. Also of concern are the grief and bereavement experiences of older people living in care homes. These are where many older people die and many important friendships made.

Feelings of bereavement are also reported in relation to caring for and caring about someone with dementia before death, where there may be feelings that the person known before the illness has been lost. Chapter 2 looks at specific issues surrounding dying with dementia.

## How do palliative care and gerontological care relate?

One of the strongest arguments for making palliative and supportive care services available to older people comes from the founder of the hospice movement. Indeed, Dame Cicely Saunders always made it clear that her 'vision' included older people, stating that "[palliative care] should not be a facet of oncology, but of geriatric medicine, neurology, general practice and throughout medicine" (Saunders and Baines, 1983, p 2).

Both palliative care and gerontological care developed immediately after the Second World War. This was at a time when the new NHS was promoting its aim of caring for all 'from the cradle to the grave'. Concerns about the care of people of all ages who were dying had been raised as a result of surveys commissioned by newly formed charities (Marie Curie Memorial Foundation and the Queen's Institute of District Nursing, 1952).

Both specialties are concerned with promoting quality of life, dignity and autonomy, placing importance on controlling symptoms well, while trying to avoid the overuse of medical investigations and aggressive treatment. Furthermore, both make the person and their family the unit of care and both have led the way in developing multidisciplinary and community-based models of care. However, there has been very little integration between the two, either clinically or academically. Gerontologists rarely explore end-of-life issues, perhaps partly because these do not fit comfortably with an agenda of 'positive ageing'.

## Key policy issues for older people: a synthesis of their implications for end-of-life care

There has been an upsurge of concern and interest in both the voluntary and statutory sectors in the circumstances in which older people die. However, as noted recently, while there exists "no coherent set of policies relating to death and dying per se, policies in several other spheres, including health and social care, shape and influence the circumstances of dying" (Lloyd, 2004, p 237). In March 2001, the government launched the National Service Framework (NSF) for Older People, with the aim of improving and standardising the quality of care for older people in a range of care environments. The NSF for Older People embraces the principles of dignity, autonomy and independence within its recommendations and is likely to make an important impact on care at the interface between acute, intermediate and continuing care. Its recommendations relating to end-of-life care can be found in Appendix C.

### Ageism

In spite of the intentions of the NSF for Older People (DH, 2001) to 'root out' age discrimination, many older people face insurmountable problems in accessing the care they need when facing the end of their lives. As Lloyd notes, "when equal rights of access to health care are asserted with no reference to the resource base of health care provision, the conditions are in place for discourses to develop that are antagonistic to older people" (Lloyd, 2004, p 237). These discourses include language such as referring to ill older people as 'bed blockers' and the tendency to view older people's care needs as 'social' rather than health-related, one implication of which is that many older people have to pay for the care that they need as they become more infirm. The fact that many older people in late old age are women may also contribute to this general picture.

*Whereas the state through the NHS pays for all the care needs of sufferers from, for example cancer and heart disease, people who suffer from Alzheimer's disease may get little or no help with the cost of comparable care needs. All these conditions are debilitating, but Alzheimer's disease cannot yet be cured by medical intervention. However, a mixture of all types of care, including personal care will be needed. This is directly analogous to the kinds of care provided for cancer sufferers. The latter get their care free. The former have to pay.* (Royal Commission on Long Term Care, 1999, ch 6, para 6.33)

At a more conceptual level, it has been argued that our tendency as a society to erect barriers against the fact of our own inevitable deaths means that we prefer to minimise the problems facing older people as they reach the end of their lives, since these are dangerous "reminders of our mortality" (Tallis, 1999, p 23).

Attempts to combat ageism by promoting a positive, healthier and more independent image of old age can also marginalise the needs of vulnerable older people. Indeed, a preoccupation with independence in much of the policy literature obscures any meaningful debate about how to improve the quality of life of older people facing death. In particular, we know little about the best way to preserve older people's dignity, privacy and comfort (Lloyd, 2004), while enabling choice and reducing any sense of being a burden. A key concern is the absence of older people's voices in shaping the services that are used at the end of life and the fact that many older people find that they must fit round service routines, rather than services being flexibly provided to meet individual needs. This is especially an issue for older people from minority ethnic groups who may already be disadvantaged, and whose needs are likely to particularly diverse (Rogers et al, 2000b; Henwood, 2001). While there may be a number of problems faced in developing meaningful approaches to consultation with older people, it is important that mechanisms are found that move beyond tokenism.

*Welfare is primarily for older people, half of all [social] security spending goes on them and they are the main client group of the NHS. Yet no services are designed for them, with them or by them*[4].

---

[4] 'MacTernan on politics', archive for 27 February 2003, www.communitycare.co.uk/article (accessed 18 June 2004).

## The 'mixed market' of care

Two million vulnerable adults need care and support in their daily lives, and live on the brink of illness or accidents. Two thirds of these are older people. Since 1993, with the implementation of the Community Care Act, their care is provided by a range of different funding sources – the so-called mixed market. Older people who become ill therefore fall in 'between the spaces' of health and social care agencies. A process of 'single assessment', started in April 2004, is designed to address some of these issues. However, it is being introduced in a climate where it is known that one third of new service users wait for over six weeks before receiving services and service reviews rarely take place on time (DH, 2004).

Frail and ill older people characteristically experience a pattern of short admissions to hospital for 'acute' episodes of illness interspersed with long periods of time at home or in care homes where support services are often poorly coordinated and overstretched. An emphasis on cost containment and poor commissioning and contracting practices detract from efforts to improve quality (Henwood, 2001). The Department of Health (DH, 2004) now acknowledges that even minor inputs of services at home can make the difference between an older person being able to stay in their home or leaving it for care elsewhere, and there appears to be some evidence of political will to address this issue.

Sometimes care tips over into abusive practices such as the use of physical or medical restraint (Macdonald et al, 2002). Where staff tend to be poorly trained and supported, the damaging effects of such practices may be unrecognised and difficult to root out. A history of poor investment in the environment of care (both physical and in terms of staffing and management) such that known risk factors for abuse exist unchecked seems to be a common factor in recent reports of bad practice from the Commission for Health Improvement[5]. Abuse in domiciliary settings by family members is the commonest type of abuse older people experience and may fundamentally affect the

---

[5] www.chi.gov.uk/eng/inspections.shtml (accessed 22 April 2004).

end-of-life care that older people receive. Such abuse has significant implications for policies directed at increasing the numbers of people who die at home.

## Support at home

New policy initiatives mean that home support services are more targeted than previously. However, within a resource-constrained system, this has meant that better and more comprehensive packages of help have gone to those with high levels of need at the expense of reductions in, or even removal of, preventive and low-level assistance. The number of older people receiving home care services has thus been falling steadily since 1993 (Social Services Inspectorate, 2003).

There are serious gaps in specialist services for older people with mental health problems and sensory impairments, as well as poor provision for minority groups (Social Services Inspectorate, 2003). Overall, opportunities to access home care and achieve home death are unevenly distributed along the lines of age, gender and socioeconomic status, and have an inverse relationship to the presence of other care provision (Grande et al, 1998).

In conducting this review, we have been struck by the lack of reference to end-of-life care in the policy literature. One of our recommendations is that policy makers explicitly address this in all future publications. We have chosen one publication (DH, 2004) relating to social care in England to illustrate how the likely implications of the recommendations for older adults facing death can be mapped out. (see Table 1.1)

## Long-term care

In England and Wales, 19% of all deaths take place in care homes, the very large majority being older people (ONS, 2004a). The percentage of deaths occurring in such institutions is increasing year on year. The likely long-term effects of implementation of the NSF for Older People on practices within care homes in the private and voluntary sectors are difficult to estimate. The 2000 Care Standards Act introduced a range of minimum standards

(Appendix E) that proprietors and managers of care homes must achieve from April 2002. These include minimum standards for building specifications, room occupancy, staff training and management. However, there are concerns that many homes within the independent and voluntary sectors have been forced out of business as a result of these requirements, resulting in compulsory relocation for some residents (Lowe, 2003).

All of these changes and initiatives are likely to impact upon the experiences of older people and family caregivers around and beyond the time of admission to nursing home care. The introduction of minimum standards and regulations, together with a national body (the Commission for Social Care Inspection) with responsibility for overseeing their implementation should, in the longer term, improve experiences of admission to, and life within, a care home. However, in the absence of adequate levels of government funding, some homes will inevitably close, resulting in disruption and trauma for the residents, their relatives and staff involved. In reality, inequalities and inconsistencies in standards of care are likely to persist, at least for the foreseeable future.

## Summary and recommendations

This chapter has:

- provided an overview of the picture of mortality in the UK, including causes of death;
- explained key terms, including end-of-life care, palliative care, terminal care, continuing care and supportive care;
- discussed the relationship between palliative and geriatric care;
- examined key policy issues that affect end-of-life care for older people.

## Table 1.1: Comment on policy: *All our lives: Social care in England 2002-2003*

From April 2004, the Commission for Social Care Inspection became the single inspectorate for social care aiming to promote improvements in social care. The report examined here looks at the performance and quality of social care services in England in the year 2002-03. Chapter 3, 'Staying independent', examines services for older people. Here we look at the implications of this report for end-of-life care.

| What is going well? | What is the likely impact for older people of this improvement? | What is not going so well? | What is the likely impact for older adults' experiences of end-of -life care? |
|---|---|---|---|
| More older people helped to live at home, increase in intensive care packages. | Choice and independence promoted. | Older people not well informed about entitlements. | Many do not get full entitlement so may live in poverty: a known risk factor for death. This may also affect informal carers. |
| Number of older people (over 65) admitted to residential care during 2002-03 reduced; 101 per 10,000 instead of 109 per 10,000 in 2001-02. | May mean more innovative approaches to care, which are allowing more choice of the place of care but could also be due to closure of homes. | Weaknesses and delays in assessing older people's needs and organising services for them. | Services do not meet older people's needs and may have dramatic impact in terms of reducing the chances of dying at home. Services may be provided only in an acute crisis. |
| Improved services for discharging from hospital reducing delays, due partly to good cooperation between hospitals and social services. | Targets are being met and joint working is more evident between hospitals and social services. This may mean more older people being cared for in their own home with well-organised services. | Too few people offered direct payments to purchase their care themselves. | Choice is compromised and commissioners/service providers make choices on behalf of older people. Lack of information of available services means that decisions may be ill-informed. |
| Social services are working with housing to provide innovative extra care housing schemes in which people needing intensive support can continue to live independently. | Reduce number of admissions to residential care and hospitals; promote independence and increase quality of life. | Continuing closures are creating shortage of places in some regions, reducing the choices available. | Lack of choice and distress if older people need to be moved. End-of-life care may be given in a location a long way from known community and family. |
| | | Mental health needs require considerable further improvement. | Mental health services for older people are already seen as the 'Cinderella of a Cinderella service'. Dementia is under-recognised as a type of terminal illness that causes much suffering. |
| | | Lack of small-scale support at very local level for transport, community activities, adaptations and equipment can reduce people's ability to lead a full and active life. | The quality of life of older people is affected; this may cause decline in health due to lack of social contact. Social isolation is a risk factor for death, and will compromise quality of life during dying. |

*Source:* DH (2004)

Key recommendations arising from these discussions include:

- Recognising better end-of-life care for older adults as an urgent public health issue, in keeping with the stance of the WHO towards palliative care. A helpful step would be to map out the variety of service provision, resources and models of care that are relevant to the end-of-life care of older adults, and to facilitate dialogue about how best to mobilise scarce resources in pursuit of better end-of-life care for us all.

- Ensuring all policy recommendations for older adults are scrutinised with a view to their implications for end-of-life care. There is currently a profound lack of consideration of such issues across the policy spectrum.

- Establishing a cross-agency collaboration to address the issues of end-of-life care for older adults. It is encouraging to note the gradual emergence of this issue onto the agenda of a range of contributors to policy making. There is an opportunity for these agencies to lead the way in demonstrating how collaboration, communication and cross-agency working can be facilitated, and to work towards the implementation of practical solutions to address what are fundamental inadequacies in end-of-life care for older adults.

- Ensuring greater collaboration between palliative care and geriatric medicine/ gerontology. This could be addressed academically through arranging symposia on end-of-life issues for older people at both palliative care and gerontology conferences, holding joint seminars and identifying research funding that could stimulate such multidisciplinary collaboration. Clinically, joint education initiatives and interdisciplinary training posts could be established.

# 2

# Patterns, circumstances and experiences of end-of-life care among older people

## Changes in the demography of ageing

The proportion of older people in UK population is growing due to falling fertility rates, the post-Second World War 'baby boom' and socioeconomic, environmental and medical improvements that have resulted in the concentration of death as an event at the end of a very long life. In describing the essential elements of demographic change in the UK, we draw on the work done by the Royal Commission on Long Term Care (Royal Commission on Long Term Care, 1999) and the Debate of the Age Group, established by Age Concern (Debate of the Age Health and Care Study Group, 1999, p 13) in which the following are highlighted:

- one person in six in the UK is aged at least 65 and by 2031 this will be true of one in four;
- almost half of the older population is aged at least 75 and the most rapid increases are among the very oldest cohorts;
- between 2001 and 2041, the numbers of people in the UK aged at least 85 are expected to double from 1.1 million to 2.3 million.

While the UK is facing a smaller change in the proportion of its older population than other developed countries, the health and care implications of population ageing are significant for UK policy. Most importantly, there needs to be changes in attitudes, service delivery and policy direction to meet the opportunities that the demographic changes present and in order to make our experience of extra years of life in older age positive and fulfilling (Debate of the

Age Health and Care Study Group, 1999). This is something that is of grave importance to us all.

Of those who are 65 now, many can expect to live for another 20 or 30 years. Old age is therefore rather meaningless as a term, and needs to be categorised into smaller age groups:

- the 'young old': ages 65-74 years;
- the 'old old': ages 75-84 years;
- the 'oldest old': 85 years and over.

There are a number of well-recognised problems in this chronological categorisation of older age. An alternative scheme has been offered by the National Service Framework for Older People (see Box 2.1).

Choosing 65 as the start of older age is linked to the social transition of retirement, when it is normally expected that active economic life will end. This is a very simplistic assumption: of course, many older people continue to be economically active in a variety of ways. Others may have retired in their early fifties and taken opportunities to change to a new career, perhaps working part time or in a voluntary capacity. The widely accepted assumption that older people are an economic 'burden' must therefore be looked at very critically.

In general terms, each cohort of older people has different social characteristics. These will change over time. Currently, many of the 'young old' are recently retired, may be wealthier than other groups of older people and with more surviving relatives and friends. Nearly

## Box 2.1: An alternative view of older age

Entering old age:  These are people who have completed their career in paid employment and/or child rearing. This is a socially constructed definition of old age, which, according to different interpretations, includes people as young as 50, or from the official retirement ages of 60 for women and 65 for men. These people are active and independent and many remain so into late old age.

- Transitional phase: This group of older people are in transition between healthy, active life and frailty. This transition often occurs in the seventh or eighth decades but can occur at any stage of older age.
- Frail older people: These people are vulnerable as a result of health problems such as stroke or dementia, social care needs or a combination of both. (DH, 2001, p 9)

three times as many women survive to late old age[1], but many women in this age group may not have married because of wartime losses, or will have experienced early widowhood. One study (Cartwright, 1993), where family or formal carers of 639 deceased patients were interviewed, found that one fifth of women aged over 85 had never married, and of these, some had no relatives at all to care for them.

A significant proportion of people in late old age live in poverty and up to one fifth live in poor housing (Office of the Deputy Prime Minister, 1998). Many do not claim the benefits to which they are entitled. In spite of this, 50% of all pensioner households draw on state benefits for half of their income; this includes their state pension (DWP, 2002). People in late old age are much more likely than younger people to be disabled by physical or mental illness due, in part, to the previous disadvantages in terms of life chances and environmental factors that they have faced. People reaching late old age, especially those who are childless, tend also to

have a rapidly diminishing social network as their surviving friends and family predecease them.

The increase in the percentage of older people who live alone has significantly increased. In northern Europe, 30-40% of all older people live alone. By the age of 75, half of all people live alone, with more women (60%) than men (33%) living this way (National Statistics, 2004). By contrast, at the end of the Second World War only one in eight older persons lived alone. Now, older people generally wish to stay in their own homes and regard either living with their children or in institutional care as unfavourable in comparison. Smaller family sizes, and changes in working patterns with more women in middle age working, contribute to this trend.

Generally, minority ethnic populations in the UK have a younger age structure. In the largest minority group, African Carribean, 15% of people are aged over 65 years.

### Ageing is everyone's concern

*We're the oldest society that's ever existed, we live longer than people have ever lived before and that has two effects. It gives enormous opportunity, but it also puts us into quite a new world. A new world, where, if you are in your twenties ... a fifth of the time in front of you is going to be spent in retirement. If you're in your thirties it goes up to a quarter. And in your forties, it's a third or a half.... I have a slogan here: "Live in the presence of all your future selves"[2].*

## Implications for health and illness

There have been a number of debates about the implications of population ageing for incidence of illness and disease among older people. The Royal Commission on Long Term Care examined the evidence, and came down in support of the 'compression of morbidity thesis', that "the factors which are causing us to live

---

[1] 'Population by age and gender', www.statistics.gov.uk (accessed 19 May 2004).

[2] 'The ageing future', Peter Laslett, www.bbc.co.uk/ worldservice/education/aspectsofage (accessed May 2004).

longer are also resulting in extra years of life free from severe disability" (Royal Commission on Long Term Care, 1999, para 2.33, cited in Debate of the Age Health and Care Study Group, 1999, p 14).

The Debate of the Age Health and Care Study Group, established by Age Concern to promote an understanding of ageing and its affects, has argued that we understand little about the strategies with which we need to engage to sustain and accelerate the compression of morbidity and to improve the quality of life for older people once they face illness. They recommend that compression of morbidity be adopted as an explicit objective of health policy, and that efforts be enhanced to understand the experience of chronic disease in older age, the factors that alleviate suffering and allow people to live more comfortably and independently (Debate of the Age Health and Care Study Group, 1999, p 15).

## Older adults and chronic illness

In the few paragraphs that follow, we draw (unless otherwise indicated) on data from the General Household Survey of 2002, published in 2004 (National Statistics, 2004).

In the UK, almost two thirds of those over the age of 75 report at least one self-reported long-standing illness. Self-reported illness is based on the respondent's own assessment of their health and therefore an increase in reported prevalence may reflect changes in health expectations that people have as well as changes in the actual prevalence of sickness. One half of over-75s report that their lifestyle is limited because of illness. Men are more likely than women to report conditions relating to the heart and circulatory system, while women are more likely to report complaints relating to the musculoskeletal system. In a study based on interviews and questionnaires of 200 people over 90 (Bury and Holme, 1991), the main impairments, reported by men and women as causing significant ill-health and reduced quality of life, were visual problems and deafness, reported by nearly half the sample population for both problems. Box 2.2 summarises the major findings relating to health and illness of

> **Box 2.2: Some main findings from the General Household Survey 2002**
>
> - The prevalence of long-standing illness, disabilities or infirmities increased from 15% of those aged under five, to 72% of those aged 75 and over.
> - The increase in prevalence was particularly marked for those aged 45 and over.
> - Between 2001 and 2002, the proportion of those with a long-standing illness increased from 63% to 72%.
> - The proportion reporting a limiting condition increased from 4% of children under five, to 53% of those aged 75 and over.
> - One in 10 (11%) of respondents under the age of 45 reported a limiting long-standing illness compared with just over a third (35%) of older respondents.
>
> *Source:* National Statistics (2004)

the General Household Survey conducted in 2002.

As the incidence of many major diseases increases with age, some older people develop multiple coexisting conditions, each requiring a range of medications for their management. Reported ill-health has been found to be a reliable indicator of health status and is an accurate predictor of early mortality, psychological health and hospital use. However, using these data to gain an insight into the incidence of chronic conditions and their consequences among older people may be problematic. Census data for 2001 show that the prevalence of chronic conditions is highest among those living in communal establishments, but the General Household Survey only surveys people living in private accommodation. Many people aged over 65 will *under*-report disabilities or chronic illness, since they associate these as a normal part of growing old. It is likely, then, that the true incidence of need among older people is higher than is apparent at first sight.

Chronic illness is unevenly distributed through the older population, with inequality in health status as a result of social class, and other sociodemographic distinctions, such as ethnicity and gender, widespread. Income, education, lifestyle, material and social resources all make a difference to the incidence of chronic illness and men and women from lower social classes more likely to report these. Geographical factors are also important. Wales, Cornwall and the coastal areas of the UK (National Statistics Online, 2004), have the highest proportions of older people, and are therefore likely to need to pay special attention to the plans in place to manage the consequences of chronic ill-health. In England, people in the Northern and Yorkshire regions reported significantly higher amounts of long-standing illnesses, limiting conditions and restricted activities (National Statistics, 2004).

As highlighted in paragraph 1.1 (Secretary of State for Health, 1999), the chances of living well into late old age depend on all of these factors and the poorer you are, the more likely you are to be ill and die younger . Poverty and poor living conditions increase with age[3], with the most severe deprivation experienced by pensioners living alone who are mainly dependent on state pensions. For these adults, almost half of their expenditure goes on housing, fuel and food[4]. Clearly, this is in part a cohort effect; but ill health aggravates poverty, which makes dying well hard to achieve.

## Implications for the provision of help and care at home

Older adults with chronic life-limiting illness or those who are frail because of advanced old age need help if they are to live at home in some degree of comfort. The availability of a family member or friend who can deliver care and help at home is thus a key factor in determining how well older people manage at home, and can be a critical factor in eventually enabling death

---

[3] Table 7: Proportion of pensioner units with less than 50% of income from state benefits 1994/5, 2000/1, p 43, www.dwp.gov.uk/asd/asd6/pi_series_001.pdf (accessed 21 May 2004).

[4] Table 4.2: Expenditure of one person retired households mainly dependent on state pensions by gross income quintile group 2001-2–2002-3, p 74, www.statistics.gov.uk/downloads/theme_social/Family_Spending_2002-3.pdf (accessed 21 May 2004).

at home. Smaller family sizes, fewer numbers of middle-aged women who have traditionally filled the caring and helping role, and larger numbers of people in full-time employment are all challenges to the provision of informal care. But lack of support for informal caregivers is perhaps an even bigger concern (Griffin, 1991). Two surveys (Cartwright et al, 1973; Seale and Cartwright, 1994) give a comprehensive picture of the way society, in the 1970s and 1980s, cared for a predominantly old and sick group of people in the year before they died. They revealed a series of inadequacies in terms of service coverage, coordination and communication. There was a lack of practical, social and emotional support for relatives and friends who had cared for people who had died. Moreover, domiciliary support in the form of home helps and district nurses was found to be sparse, and was conjoined with limited bed availability, both in hospitals and in other institutions.

### Care giving in illness: the experience of 'muddling through'

*Carers generally felt neglected in terms of the amount and continuity of support they received, although their contact with particular individuals was usually reported favourably. Isolation, a fervent desire to carry on 'coping', coupled with a sense of having to muddle through with support that was barely adequate, often unsuitable, and difficult to find out about was prevalent.* (Seymour and Hanson, 2000, p 107)

It is a well-known, but under-recognised, fact that many of those who provide help, care and support to an older neighbour, friend or relative (often a spouse) are themselves of older age. The demands on older spouses, friends or other relatives of ill older adults are likely to increase as the proportion of working age people declines (Davies and Higginson, 2004a).

### Facing death in old age: the broad picture

#### *The average age of death*

As we enter the middle of the first decade of the 21st century, life expectancy for both

**Table 2.1: Major cause of death: by sex and age, 2002 (%)**

| England and Wales | 50-64 | Men 65-84 | 85+ | 50-64 | Women 65-84 | 85+ |
|---|---|---|---|---|---|---|
| Cancers | 39 | 32 | 18 | 53 | 29 | 12 |
| Circulatory system | 36 | 42 | 42 | 22 | 40 | 44 |
| Digestive system | 7 | 4 | 3 | 6 | 5 | 4 |
| Respiratory system | 7 | 13 | 19 | 8 | 13 | 17 |
| Injury and poisoning | 4 | 1 | 2 | 3 | 1 | 2 |
| Nervous system | 2 | 3 | 3 | 3 | 3 | 3 |
| Mental and behavioural | 1 | 1 | 3 | – | 2 | 6 |
| Other | 4 | 5 | 9 | 5 | 7 | 14 |
| All deaths (=100%) (000s) | 35.6 | 144.6 | 53.6 | 23.0 | 129.6 | 116.3 |

*Source:* National Statistics Online (2004)

men and women continues to rise, with latest statistics indicating that, in 2002, life expectancy at birth for women born in the UK was 81 years, and 76 years for men. This contrasts with 49 and 45 years respectively in 1901. In 2002, women aged 65 could expect to live up to the age of 84, while men of the same age could expect to live to 81. Death rates for those reaching 80 years of age have been rapidly declining, with more people surviving into their hundreds. Even for someone reaching their 100th birthday, the probability of dying within 12 months is less than one in two (National Statistics Online, 2004).

## Causes of death among older adults

Older people die from the same diseases as younger people, although the proportions dying of cancer as a primary cause decrease with age and the proportions dying from circulatory and/or respiratory diseases as primary causes increase. Dementia is an important and increasing cause of death among older people, but it is infrequently recorded as a primary cause of death. This means that there tends to be a lack of recognition of the terminal nature of the condition in its advanced stages and a lack of forward planning in considering the needs that patients and their carers are likely to have as the disease progresses. Of course, as we note above, older people often have more than one major disease when they die and it can be difficult to ascertain which led most directly to

death. Table 2.1 summarises the major causes of death by sex and age during 2002.

## Place of death among older adults

Among people of all ages, approximately 56% of deaths occur in hospital, 19% at home, 18% in a care home and 4% in a hospice (National Statistics, 2003). About half of all deaths do not take place in the setting that the dying person prefers, which for more than half of us is at home (Higginson, 2003). There is considerable geographical variation in the numbers of deaths that occur at home, indicating that organisation of services plays a major role in determining the possibilities for place of death. There are also gender differences: among men, in 2001, 22% of those who died did so in their own homes, while only 4% died in communal establishments. For women, these figures are 16% and 11% respectively, reflecting women's longer life expectancy and increased likelihood of living in a care home in later life (National Statistics, 2003).

A study of trends in place of death among patients with cancer over the 10-year period 1985-94 (Higginson et al, 1998) shows that, across all regions in England, older people with cancer are less likely to die at home than younger people; this is particularly the case for people aged over 85 years who are most likely to die in communal establishments (largely care homes). Indeed, only 8.5% of those aged over 85 dying of cancer die in a hospice, compared

## Table 2.2: Place of death in England and Wales (2001) – all ages (%)

| Setting | Deaths at all ages | Over 65 years | 85+ |
|---|---|---|---|
| Home | 19 | 17 | 11 |
| NHS hospitals and NHS nursing homes | 56 | 56 | 51 |
| Voluntary hospices | 4 | 4 | 1 |
| Communal establishments | 18 | 21 | 36 |

*Source:* National Statistics Online (2004)

with 20% of all cancer deaths (National Statistics, 2003). These figures are mirrored in place of death for all ages and causes and remained broadly stable into 2001 as shown in Table 2.2.

Studies carried out in Europe and the US find similar trends, with a difference between the number of older adults wishing to die at home and actually dying at home, and evidence that those in late old age who are female and unmarried are least likely to die at home (Klinkenberg, 2003).

## Older adults' last year of life: quality of life, needs and symptoms

Little is known about older adults' experiences of the last year of their life: the evidence that we do have has been gathered largely from bereaved family members, who were asked to report on the older person's needs during the months before death. In a report for the World Health Organization about the palliative care needs of older people Davies and Higginson (2004a, section 2, pp 14-15), draw attention to the following as being of particular importance:

- Many older people have multiple medical problems.
- The cumulative effects of these lead to greater impairment and needs for care than would be the case for any individual condition.
- Older people are at greater risk of complications from treatment, including adverse drug reactions.
- Older people who are ill are likely to have increased psychological distress.
- Older people may experience episodes of acute illness against a backdrop of social isolation, physical or mental impairment, and economic hardship.

### Ageing and dying are interlinked

*The problems that many older people experience in the last year of life are therefore those of great age and its troubles as well as those caused by a final illness.* (Davies and Higginson, 2004a, section 2, p 15)

### *The empirical evidence: an overview*

In the early 1990s, Seale and Cartwright (1994) interviewed the bereaved companions or relatives of a sample of 800 people who had died during one year in 10 areas of England. In a similar study in the 1990s, Addington-Hall and McCarthy (1995) surveyed 4,000 companions of a random sample of people who died in 20 areas of the UK.

Seale and Cartwright (1994) demonstrated that the older people who died within their sample were more likely to be women, less likely to be married and less likely to have living relatives on whom to rely for informal care. People aged 85 years and older were especially disadvantaged in terms of family support, but were not receiving more attention from general practitioners or community nurses, even though those dying after the age of 85 were least likely to be admitted to a hospital or hospice during the last year of their lives. In contrast, among people aged between 65-85, the majority of deaths occurred within hospitals, in spite of the acknowledged preference among the majority of older people to remain at home. Overall, Seale and Cartwright calculate that 22% of 'bed days' are used by those in the last year of their lives, and that the majority of these are used by older age groups.

Seale and Cartwright's analysis suggests that these trends were particularly marked among older people who had died from diseases other than cancer. These people suffered longer periods of dependency and illness than cancer sufferers and received care that was comparatively poorly coordinated. Older people, particularly those with non-cancer palliative care needs, were "relatively neglected in relation to care and research" (Seale and Cartwright, 1994, p 87), and it seemed that there existed a law of 'inverse care':

> The most disconcerting finding from this study is the lack of responsiveness of the medical and nursing services to the needs of older people in the last year of their lives. (Seale and Cartwright, 1994, p 93)

Addington-Hall and McCarthy (1995) examined the prevalence of physical symptoms and pain among dying people and the types of services they received, publishing valuable information about the circumstances of people dying from cancer, heart disease, stroke and dementia. In a detailed comparison of cancer and non-cancer deaths (Addington-Hall et al, 1998), they concluded that:

- one in six non-cancer patients experiences symptoms such as pain and breathlessness that are similar to those experienced by the most severely affected cancer patients;
- specialist palliative care services are almost exclusively delivered to those with cancer;
- it is likely that 71,744 people who die from non-malignant disease in England and Wales each year have specialist palliative care needs, and that these people are, on average, from older age groups than those with similar levels of need in the cancer population.

A local needs assessment (Skilbeck et al, 1997) of patients with chronic obstructive pulmonary disease – most of whom were older people – found a group of people who were extremely disabled and had a number of severe symptoms, including pain and breathlessness. Professional care tended to be focused on those occasions when they became acutely ill, with needs for social support, respite and future planning poorly addressed.

While there are clearly differences between individual diseases, many symptoms and problems people face in the last year of life are similar (Higginson, 1997). Moreover, families and friends will face similar issues in trying to help and support older adults during this last phase of life. However, most of the research that has been done to understand the experience of living with advanced illness has focused on cancer: we know comparatively little about the experience of living with diseases other than cancer, and even less about the particular issues that may face older adults and their families and friends. However, uncertainty, anxiety and depression, and difficulties in anticipating, planning and accessing health and social support services may be significant problems.

## The individual nature of needs

> Concerns and the interpretation of terms such as 'quality of life' are highly individual. Some people are most concerned about physical symptoms such as pain, and some by the effect the illness has on their everyday life. Others may be distressed by the uncertainty of their situation, by religious or spiritual concerns or by the effect of their illness on their family. Patients' views can be different from those of their health professionals, and different in turn from those of the family member caring for them. (Davies and Higginson, 2004b, p 12)

Under-assessment and under-treatment of problems, especially pain, together with great variations in the quality of information, degree of involvement in decision making and supportive care interventions, have been found in large studies of seriously ill older people in the US (Lynn et al, 1997). These are likely to be applicable to the UK context. The next chapter examines in greater detail some of these issues and how they relate to different settings of care.

Here, attention turns to focus on two conditions from which older people suffer commonly: dementia and heart disease. We have chosen to emphasise these since there are clear and acknowledged inequalities in the end-of-life care that adults with dementia receive, and because heart disease is likely to become the leading cause of death for older people by 2020.

We also examine the situation of people in very late old age, looking at the evidence that exists about this stage of life. Of course, our separation of these three is artificial: late old age is often a time when a number of chronic diseases, such as dementia and heart disease, combine to cause an interconnected range of physical, psychological and social problems.

# Dementia

Dementia is a term used to describe a range of conditions in which the brain has been damaged, affecting memory, mood and concentration. Approximately 700,000 people have dementia in the UK (Wasson et al, 2001). The disease is progressive and although it mainly affects older people, younger people can also be affected. Over the age of 65 years, dementia affects four to five people in every hundred. Over the age of 80 years, the incidence rises to one in five adults. Although the risk rises with age, the majority of 90-year-olds are unaffected. A study of prevalence of dementia across Europe shows that 4% of people aged over 70 are affected by dementia, increasing to 13% of those over 80 (Hofman et al, 1991).

The two main types of dementia are Alzheimer's disease and vascular dementia. Alzheimer's disease is characterised by the presence of plaques in brain tissues. It is the commonest cause of dementia but how it develops is poorly understood. While there is no cure for Alzheimer's disease, in some people the progression of the disease can be slowed by the use of drugs known as 'cognitive enhancers'; these were recommended for prescription by the National Institute of Clinical Excellence in tightly defined circumstances, although this recommendation is under review. Vascular dementia (also called multi-infarct dementia) is caused by an impairment of the blood supply to the brain and takes a number of different forms.

In its advanced stages, dementia is characterised by increasing dependency on others for care, although there may be a loss of recognition of loved ones, which is very distressing both for the sufferer and their caregivers. However, most people with dementia retain a capacity for non-verbal communication, a desire to make their own choices and sensitivity to the emotions of others. More than 95% of dementia sufferers will need 24-hour care at the end of their lives (Lloyd-Williams and Payne, 2002).

### Where do people with dementia die and what do they die of?

The median length of survival from diagnosis of dementia to death is eight years, and ability, awareness and symptom load (for example, confusion, incontinence, pain, distress, problems with sleeping and eating) increase gradually over this period (Van der Steen et al, 2002). The symptoms that adults with dementia have are similar to those of adults with advanced cancer, but in dementia they last longer and levels of care needed are often higher (McCarthy et al, 1997a).

Three key scenarios have been identified for adults dying with dementia (Cox and Cook, 2002):

- People who live with dementia but die from some other identifiable primary condition (such as cancer) before their dementia is far advanced.
- People whose death occurs because of a complex mix of problems before their dementia is far advanced.
- People who die of the complications of end-stage dementia, such as brain failure and pneumonia.

Adults with dementia tend to be older than those dying from cancer, and are more likely to have spent the last year of life in a care home. They are less likely than people with other diseases to be admitted to hospital or a hospice in the last year of life (McCarthy et al, 1997a). Some adults with dementia will die in their own homes being cared for by close family. In these incidences, getting access to NHS-funded care packages or specialist palliative care is both rare and difficult. GPs and district nurses are less involved in the care of adults with dementia than those dying from other conditions, and families report concerns about their GP's understanding of dementia, as well as the quality of information provided to them about dementia and about how to care for their relative (McCarthy et al, 1997a).

Informal carers of people with dementia are less likely than carers of people with other diseases to report that they find caring rewarding, although there is evidence that they take opportunities to find social and practical help from dedicated support groups where these exist in their area (McCarthy et al, 1997a). The consequences of these problems for the quality of care that people with dementia receive, and the impact on the health, well-being and bereavement of their family, is significant. Families have to cope with inexorably increasing and changing needs for care, as well as the sadness of losing the ability to communicate with their relative. This has been described as a living bereavement. Box 2.3 summarises some experiences of caring for people who die from dementia.

### Key issues related to dying with dementia

Deaths in which dementia is the primary or contributory cause are marked by uncertainty. Questions about when the dying phase has been entered, how symptoms (such as pain) should be assessed and managed when communication is no longer possible with the person, decisions about the cessation or continuation of medical treatments, particularly where these involve artificial feeding or hydration, and issues about the place in which the person should be cared for – all of these are complex and difficult to address.

### Assessing pain and other symptoms

A retrospective study on a ward for older people with mental health needs in the UK (Lloyd-Williams and Payne, 2002) showed that patients with end-stage dementia had a number of symptoms for which they did not receive effective palliative care. In particular, analgesia was infrequently used. In some cases, the dying phase was not recognised and some patients were given, probably inappropriately, intravenous antibiotics in the last few days of life. One of the debates about care for patients with advanced dementia is whether withholding antibiotic treatment for terminal illnesses such as pneumonia makes their dying more or less distressing (Van der Steen et al, 2002). Clearly,

no blanket policy can be advised, but whether antibiotics are used or not, any patients who appear to be suffering must receive, as a priority, palliative care that addresses symptomatic relief in accordance with standards of best practice. In the study by Lloyd-Williams and Payne (2002), guidelines were developed in conjunction with a palliative care specialist to help ward-based medical staff. An audit of patients' notes before and a year after the implementation of the guidelines indicated that:

- there was an increase in the use of analgesics, including opiates, although the use of syringe drivers was still low;
- there was a large decrease in the use of antibiotics in the last two weeks of life.

A number of authors discuss problems of pain assessment and management in advanced dementia care. Pain perception is altered in dementia and can, in some cases, be heightened. One report (Kovach et al, 1999) of an intervention designed to assess and treat pain and discomfort (the Assessment of Discomfort in Dementia (ADD) Protocol) suggests a useful approach to these issues and demonstrates that the needs of people with advanced dementia can be discerned and treated. The tool guides the user through a physical and medical assessment of possible sources of pain and discomfort and then through other factors, including emotional sources of distress. Alongside this, pharmacological and non-pharmacological comfort measures are suggested. Symptoms of pain and discomfort (sad facial expression, tense body language, fidgeting, perseverant verbalisations, verbal outbursts, and so on) were significantly decreased following the introduction of the assessment tool. Regular analgesic prescriptions increased during this time but the use of intermittent analgesia or psychotropic medication 'as required' did not. Using such assessment tools is important, although further research to enable precise discrimination between discomfort and suffering due to pain or due to other symptoms is required, to ensure that the appropriate medical or nursing interventions can be delivered.

## Box 2.3: Carers' experiences of looking after people who die from dementia

Struggles to care

- "I think what makes it so difficult for people to carry on caring at home is that services are so disjointed ... you're lost in a sea of people. You don't [know] who's meant to be doing what."
- "One night, Mum was so bad I thought as though I couldn't continue any more." I 'phoned a voluntary worker, really only just to talk to her because I knew she would listen. It was 10 o'clock at night and she just said 'I'm on my way', and she was wonderful."
- "It's just having someone to talk to who knows what [you] are going through."
- "If I hadn't have had the district nurses many a time – 'cos [Mum] kept having little strokes and you – I mean that's another thing, it would be smashing if we had some kind of training because I didn't know what to look for initially and when she did have a stroke I panicked, thinking what do I do? Do I phone 999? Or, as the doctor said in the end, just try and put an aspirin in her mouth and let her sleep through it because what will they do if they take her in hospital? But I didn't know what to look for and I panicked because I knew she wasn't right."
- "[My husband] fell out of bed one night and I knew I couldn't get him back in."

The care home option is not a real choice; care staff are young and inexperienced

- "[I wanted to feel] that they were looking after him 100% rather than 35%. I gave him 100% of my care when he was at home ... but if it was a job they were doing they weren't doing it well, probably because of a lack of training ... there were some staff there who were 18, 19, 20 ... what they needed was someone who knew what people's needs were through experience; if they'd been taught by people with experience of looking after people in that situation the care would automatically have been better."

Dementia is not recognised as a terminal illness

- "I think the thing about dementia is that it's not classed as a terminal illness, although it does cause somebody's death and it's the beginning of the end."

An example of death managed well

- "... The doctor that was attending to him explained to us that he would not be allowed to die in pain and that they make the end peaceful and they gave him morphine ... I had spent from the morning till 10 o'clock at night the day before ... I said, 'Whatever time it is I want to be there and I want my family there as well because that is what they want'. They telephoned me at quarter past six, and that was it ... it was absolutely wonderful".

*Source:* Seymour et al (2003)

### *When the person with dementia cannot eat or drink*

Problems with eating and difficulties surrounding decisions about nutrition are common at the end of life for adults with dementia. In a report published in 2000 by the Alzheimer's Society (Alzheimer's Society, 2000), 80% of people with dementia were reported as likely to suffer from eating difficulties. These will be partly due to the effects of the disease process on appetite and the ability to swallow, but lack of carers' time, poor choices of food and lack of carers' skill and understanding are also implicated in weight loss and malnutrition among care home residents and hospital patients (Meier et al, 2001). More simply, some people who appear to retain the ability to eat and drink refuse to do so. How caregivers should respond is a matter of debate, with some saying that such refusal is an expression of individual autonomy which should be respected (Wasson et al, 2001), and others arguing that this is one manifestation of the disease process that should be managed medically, both to relieve possible hunger and thirst and extend life (Wasson et al, 2001).

The most common form of medical treatment for problems with eating and drinking is to commence artificial forms of nutrition and hydration, either intravenously or, more commonly, via the intestinal tract using tubes. However, studies conducted in non-palliative care settings have shown that, except for patients in coma, artificial hydration and feeding have no benefits, in terms of length of survival, over hand feeding (Meier et al, 2001). In patients with end-stage dementia, artificial feeding neither reduces the risk of aspiration pneumonia, infections or pressure sores; nor offsets the effects of malnutrition (Winter, 2000). Furthermore, some older people who are being artificially fed need to be restrained from pulling out their feeding tubes. This can be a significant contributor to their suffering during the final period of their lives (Peck et al, 1990) and may lead to increased use of drugs as a 'chemical cosh' (Gillick, 2000). Moreover, problems of infection and ulceration associated with feeding tubes and intravenous feeding lines are well known.

Older people living at home or in other care settings are reported to be less likely to want to have artificial feeding than other interventions, such as cardio-pulmonary resuscitation, in any clinical condition, although there are ethnic, cultural and gender variations (Blackhall et al, 1999). Preferences about life-sustaining interventions seem to be strongly related to ideas about cognitive functioning and permanence of the procedure (Cohen-Mansfield et al, 1991), or to worries about how such interventions may prolong dying and make it unnatural and undignified (Seymour, 2002).

The symbolism of food and the way in which families, doctors and nurses become involved in socially shared 'nurturing rituals' (McInerney, 1992) during the care of ill and dying people helps us to understand why, in spite of the evidence of the difficulties associated with artificial feeding, it is difficult to withhold or withdraw it from people with dementia. Carefully considering the contribution such interventions can make to the overall comfort

and quality of life of the person, ideally in conjunction with discussion with the person's family and following attempts to ascertain any wishes they may have expressed previously, is important. Ensuring that time is taken to sit with the person and offer oral fluids and ice, or to give frequent mouth care, is mandatory.

> ### Box 2.4: A widower's account of his wife's death
>
> *Harry: "I suppose these last three years, she couldn't talk, she'd no co-ordination, she couldn't swallow, she was fed by PEG\*, we had a hospital bed, yeah, she wasn't incontinent but she couldn't tell us she wanted to go to the toilet so she had to be incontinent, she used to go in respite care for a fortnight every six weeks and then in February she went in, in [hospital] and they decided that I shouldn't cope any longer and they kept her in the rehab unit which I think was the wrong place because she was really, it's a terminal illness.... I used to go to bed at night and say, "I hope to God she's not here tomorrow morning", and I did that for two years, you know, it was awful really, 'cause she wasn't even existing. Unfortunately she knew what was going off, she could hear, and with that complaint your hearing doesn't go I gather, it's the muscles of your throat which [meant] she couldn't swallow so she had this PEG in and then she had this machine 10 hours a day feeding her, you know.  Thankfully she died.... The last couple of weeks they more or less said the only thing that was keeping her alive is her feeding 'cause she was fed by PEG; you know, pump and PEG. And she had that for three years. So nothing went through her mouth, it was one heck of a job ... she was on this machine 10 hours a day, she'd go on when the carers came in the morning at half past nine and they'd take it off when they came at night at half past seven and I didn't mind. But then I used to think, it's all of these things keeping her alive! She wasn't on any treatment because there wasn't any treatment ... so you know it was hell for her really."*
>
> \* Percutaneous Endoscopic Gastrostomy tube
> *Source:* Seymour et al (2003)

## Making care and treatment decisions

In dementia, there comes a time when the person can no longer make decisions or express wishes about their care and treatment. In the UK there is comparatively little use of advance statements, which allow people to express wishes about how they wish decisions to be made about their care or to make an advance refusal of life-prolonging interventions such as artificial feeding. We examine these in Chapter 4. Suffice to say here that the general difficulty in establishing the wishes of people with dementia means that they are vulnerable to both over- and under-treatment, especially where opportunities have not been taken to discuss prognostic and diagnostic information with the individual and his/her family at an earlier stage. At the moment, decision making at the end of life is the responsibility of medical practitioners, although key guidance (BMA, 2001; GMC, 2002) states that they must consult with those who know the individual well once the person concerned can no longer represent themselves. This may be relatives or other care staff. One of the key difficulties here is that patients with dementia will often not have access to medical staff who know them well. Doctors may therefore react to individual problems at the end of life rather than making an ongoing assessment of the person's situation and care.

A study from the US of four nursing homes (Forbes et al, 2000) provides some evidence of the issues that family members consider important in end-of-life care and decision making for people with dementia. Findings show a lack of knowledge about the dying process in dementia, with many participants not recognising the advancing symptoms of dementia (deteriorating cognition, swallowing problems, repeated infections) as signs of approaching death. Many talked in terms of contributing to end-of-life decisions 'when the need arose', but did not understand clearly when that might occur. Involvement in decision making for the person with dementia was seen as an 'emotional burden' that compounded the guilt already felt from the need for the person to enter the care home. Although participants were clear that they did not want to prolong suffering, they were also worried about being an 'agent of death'. Death was perceived as more acceptable if a doctor had told them that the illness was terminal. 'Peace of mind' was the implicit goal of most family members in trying to decide what was best for the person with dementia.

> *Torn between death as an acceptable blessing versus a forbidden tragedy, family members did not want to be an 'agent of death'. Family members wanted peace of mind, to believe that they had done everything possible and that death was beyond their control.* (Forbes et al, 2000, p 253)

> *For these family members, decision-making might be compared to travelling on a long, arduous and unwelcome journey. The diagnosis and progression of the dementia-related illness forced participants into a scenario that they did not request or desire, embarking on a journey in the land of death, filled with intense emotional pain and conflict.* (Forbes et al, 2000, p 254)

## Heart failure

Heart failure (HF), in which either the heart muscle or the valves of the heart no longer function well, is mainly a disease of older people. Its prevalence rises exponentially with age from 5.5 per 1,000 population for people in their 50s, to 47 per 1,000 for those in their 80s (Jones et al, 2003). Sixty thousand deaths a year are attributed to heart failure, although advances in medical treatment have resulted in a decrease in early mortality with a corresponding increase in the numbers surviving with disabilities (Ward, 2002). HF has a poor prognosis, with 62% surviving one year after diagnosis for all ages. HF has a worse prognosis than several major cancers, including bowel cancer in men and breast cancer in women (DH, 2000b). The major morbidity and mortality associated with HF means that it has become a focus of policy attention, with a National Service Framework dedicated to heart disease published in 2000 (DH, 2000b). This makes explicit reference to the need to take a palliative care perspective to the care of people with advanced disease. However, only a tiny number of referrals of patients with HF are made to specialist palliative care services (0.3 % of domiciliary referrals, 0.4% of inpatient referrals). This compares with 56% of cancer patients receiving some care from specialists (Ward, 2002). The unpredictable nature of HF, which can worsen and improve in cycles over time, is one factor that makes planning for care difficult.

## The palliative care needs of adults with heart failure

*The palliative care needs of patients living with heart failure are similar to those living with cancer and yet there are fewer services available to them. Physicians and other health professionals need to be aware that these patients may benefit from referral to specialist palliative care services.* (Horne and Payne, 2004, p 296)

### Living in the last year of life with heart failure: symptoms and problems

UK research into the needs and experiences of people with HF has mainly been conducted retrospectively, and shows that people with HF experience difficulties in accessing information about their illness or what choices may be made in relation to their care (McCarthy et al, 1997b; Rogers et al, 2000a). In the Regional Study of the Care of the Dying (McCarthy et al, 1996), data were gathered from the bereaved next of kin of 675 adults who had died of HF in 20 health districts. Relatives were asked to report on the needs and symptoms of the person during their last year of life. Many patients were reported as having been unable to get adequate information about their condition, and of those who were thought to have known they were dying, 82% were reported to have worked this out for themselves. A wide range of symptoms were reported, including pain, breathlessness, low mood and anxiety. These were frequently distressing and lasted in many cases for longer than six months. For more than a quarter of patients, management in hospital brought no or little relief. At the time of death, 54% of patients died in hospital, 30% in their own home and 11% in a care home. More than one third of people died without their relative present. These findings broadly correspond with results from a large study conducted in the US (Levenson et al, 2000). Box 2.5 summarises key points from an assessment for the need for a palliative care approach among patients with HF.

### Experiences of living with and being treated for heart failure

Many people with HF have a variety of coexisting conditions, such as chronic obstructive pulmonary disease, arthritis or diabetes. Such individuals have to live with the profound psychological and social effects that chronic illness has on their lives; they must also manage the side-effects of multiple medications and deal with the uncertainty of whether or not they will cope with each new day. Moreover, fatigue is also a significant, but probably under-recognised issue for people living with HF (Jones at al, 2003; Horne and Payne, 2004). In the needs assessment study referred to earlier (Ward, 2002), 60% of patients with HF attending an outpatient clinic reported that one or more of their problems were inadequately addressed, often because they had concerns that were not directly related to their cardiac condition. Adding the simple question 'what are your three most troublesome symptoms?' to the assessment process was found to enable many patients to talk about problems that they previously did not raise with their doctors (Ward, 2002).

---

### Box 2.5: Key issues: heart failure and palliative care

- A strategy is needed to ensure a timely and progressive move away from invasive treatment and towards supportive terminal care for patients with HF.
- The views of HF patients on how they would prefer to be treated are often not sought.
- Palliative care specialists have developed treatment strategies that effectively control many of the distressing symptoms reported by HF patients at the end of life.
- The basic principles of palliative care – good communication and close attention to symptom control – should be adopted to improve the quality of life of HF patients.

*Source:* Adapted from Ward (2002)

Further evidence about the experiences and concerns of people with HF is available from a comparative study (Murray et al, 2002) of the experience of 20 cancer and 20 HF patients and their carers who were interviewed at three-monthly intervals for one year. The interviewees with HF had an average age of 75, while the patients with cancer had an average age of 65. Almost two thirds of the interviewees in both groups died before the end of the study. Box 2.6 summarises the different experiences of the interviewees.

Two of the authors of this report (Gott and Payne) are currently engaged in a study that examines the symptoms and service use among 540 people aged over 60 years with HF. The study is funded by the Department of Health.

There is some evidence that older people with HF tend to attribute problems that they have to 'old age' and believe that 'nothing can be done'

to help. Such attitudes are compounded by the unpredictable nature of the condition and the absence of public knowledge about HF; a striking difference when compared with public awareness of cancer. Social isolation, whether caused by poverty, the limitations of the disease and its treatments, or the lack of opportunities to make any continuous relationship with a named key professional, seems to be one of the most significant factors in patients' and carers' experiences of HF (see Box 2.7).

In the study by Murray et al (2002), few patients had developed an ongoing relationship with a health professional. Contact with social services or carer support services, for example, respite, was largely absent. Similarly, information available from cardiac charities such as the British Heart Foundation was little used.

## Box 2.6: Comparison of experience of patients with heart failure and lung cancer

| Lung cancer | Cardiac failure |
|---|---|
| Cancer trajectory with clearer terminal phase; able to plan for death | Gradual decline punctuated by episodes of acute deterioration; sudden, usually unexpected death with no distinct terminal phase |
| Initially feel well but told you are ill | Feel ill but told you are well |
| Good understanding of diagnosis and prognosis | Little understanding of diagnosis and prognosis |
| "How long have I got?" | "I know it won't get better, but I hope it won't get any worse" |
| Relatives anxious | Relatives isolated and exhausted |
| Swinging between hope and despair | Daily grind of hopelessness |
| Lung cancer takes over life and becomes overriding concern | Much comorbidity to cope with; heart often not seen as main issue |
| Treatment calendar dominates life, more contact with services and professionals | Shrinking social world dominates life, little contact with health and social services |
| Feel worse on treatment: coping with side-effects | Feel better on treatment: work of balancing and monitoring in the community |
| Financial benefits accessible | Less access to benefits with uncertain prognosis |
| Specialist services often available in the community | Specialist services rarely available in the community |
| Care prioritised early as 'cancer' and later as 'terminally ill' | Less priority as a 'chronic disease' and less priority later as uncertain if yet 'terminally ill' |

*Source:* Murray et al (2002)

# Facing death in late old age: "death keeps on taking little bits of me"[5]

With longer life expectancies, more of us are living to advanced old age. Clearly, chronological age is not tied in any direct sense to biological age. Many people in their 90s are much fitter than some who are decades younger. However, for some, the awareness of mortality in late old age may be tightly tied to the frustrations of having to live with creeping infirmity and disability, and a sense in which the body becomes an unreliable vessel disconnected from the real 'self' within. For many very old people, dying is merely the protracted process of living with multiple losses: loss of social contact, physical fitness and cognition. There is often no definable moment at which 'dying' commences among very old people, and the complex factors that lead to death can only be understood retrospectively (Lloyd, 2004). It remains remarkably common, in our highly medicalised society, to use the label 'old age' as a cause of death: some 3% of all deaths in England and Wales are categorised in this way in spite of easily available evidence of comorbid conditions in those cases (see Box 2.8). There is certainly considerable evidence that the physical problems and symptoms that people have in late old age (such as confusion, vision or hearing problems) are frequently neglected and can become very distressing (Cartwright, 1993).

This tendency to attribute deaths to 'old age' reveals how, as a society, we tend to assume that such deaths are 'timely' or 'natural' (Howarth, 1998) and therefore less worthy of our time and concern than the deaths of younger people. As a result, older people are not considered to be in need of the special care or support given to younger persons facing death. It is because of this broadly cultural stance that older adults' resources (in terms of their access to health, social and informal care and their economic situation) have such a significant impact on the levels of choice, comfort and quality of life that they can achieve in the last phase of their lives (Lloyd, 2004, p 237). Inequalities in these areas draw sharp attention to the need to understand how, for older people who need help and care, their level of self-determination or autonomy depends on their ability to purchase services (Lloyd, 2004, p 240). Many older people may feel that they have fewer rights than others to call for the help and support they need, and may be reluctant therefore to accept what little help can be provided to them without costs attached.

## Box 2.7: Experiences of living with heart failure

*Researcher: "What effect has this illness had upon your life?"*
*Paula: "We can't go anywhere. I can't do much."*
*Researcher: "How do you spend your days?"*
*Paula: "Well, crosswords, jigsaw puzzles, but I can't concentrate a lot. Watch the telly, but you get fed up of watching the telly. I listen to the radio."*
*Researcher: "Do you do this together? [to Martin] "Do you join in as well?"*
*Martin: "I do, yes. But we can't go anywhere or do anything."*
(Husband and wife)

*Mary: "I rang GP who said to ring hospital, rang hospital and was told they couldn't do anything, you have to ring GP!"*
(Woman with HF)

*Source:* Aldred et al (forthcoming)

## Box 2.8: Dying of old age. An over-cited cause?

Old age is recorded as the only cause of death in up to 3% of cases in England and Wales.

In most cases, simple enquiry revealed comorbid conditions known at the time of death.

Failure to record these conditions may affect national and international health policies, investment and statistics.

*Source:* Adapted from Hawley (2003)

---

[5]   Kafetz (2003)

## The cultural roots of our attitude to death in old age

*One must look to broader cultural factors to understand why the experience of a prolonged period of deterioration and decline prior to death is seen and experienced in self-debasing ways.* (Lawton, 2000, p 173)

There is some evidence that people in late old age do not fear death per se, but rather anticipate it practically, realistically and may even joke about it with one another. One woman of almost 88 who wrote a personal reflection for Help the Aged makes this clear in her description of the lists she now leaves for friends and family to tell them the whereabouts of presents that she has recently bought for people, and when she has booked tickets for the theatre or other venues: "Why waste expensive tickets – let someone else enjoy them – makes sense to me".

## See you in the morning – if we're still here!

*"Oh yes. The lady next door, she'll be ninety-three in June, and she's full of arthritis, she's all right up here but she has arthritis and things. Oh, we often have these discussions and I say 'Goodnight' and I say, 'See you in the morning' and we both say 'If we're still here', you know and that [laughs]. So I mean it isn't ... and the state of the world today I think, you think to yourself, you'd be better out of it, I think [laughs]."* (A woman in her late 80s reflecting on death, Seymour et al, 2003)

For some, death may promise release from the confines and constraints of late old age, and an opportunity to rejoin the past, or those who have been lost (Young and Cullen, 1996). However, people in late old age are concerned about the possibility of creeping indignity, and worried about the process of dying, particularly dying alone and in pain. Most importantly, dignity, a key concept in ideas about 'good death' is fundamentally threatened where people in late old age cannot gain access to the basic elements required to enable them to live without loneliness, fear or discomfort.

## Dignity and late old age: older people's views and experiences

*Fear of accidents, fear of dying alone and fear of being forced to move into residential care were all cited as factors which adversely affect dignity. In addition, an individual's self esteem can be significantly harmed if there is little or no support to help them come to terms with losses that they might experience when treatment, care and support are needed. Such losses include those of functional ability and of memory; bereavement —whether of a partner, spouse or other relatives; losing pets, possessions and the person's own home if care in a residential setting is needed.* (King's Fund, 1999, p 8)

*Dignity was conceptualised as 'dignity as identity' (self respect, self esteem, pride, integrity, trust), 'human rights' (equality and human entitlement to dignity) and 'dignity as autonomy' (independence, self determination, freedom of choice).* (Woolhead et al, 2004, p 169)

# Summary and recommendations

This chapter has:

- Focused on changes in the demography of ageing, drawing out the implications of these for health and illness in older age.
- Explored the concepts of comorbidity and frailty in later life.
- Examined the importance of carer availability in enabling older people to live (and die) at home.
- Looked at the end-of-life experiences of older people with heart failure, dementia and those in late old age.

Key recommendations arising from these discussions include the need to:

- Recognise comorbidity and frailty in older age as key issues in older adults' experiences of end of life: disease-focused practice is outmoded and leads to socially exclusive practices, poorly integrated care and a lack of forward planning for future needs.

- Develop practical initiatives to help and support frail adults with severe chronic illnesses. These should take precedence over any concern with defining the 'dying' phase: the basis on which referral to specialist palliative care services and a range of benefits tends to be based currently.

- Initiate and develop a carer outreach scheme, perhaps using trained peer educators. This is something suggested by attendees at a consultation meeting to inform this project.

- The intersection between poverty in older age and the quality of environment and care that older adults encounter at the end of life requires close scrutiny: the specialist palliative care movement has largely ignored the material and economic influences on dying, and yet these critically shape older adults' access to the care resources that can enable 'good death'.

- Devote specific policy attention to the experience of end of life for older adults who live alone, many of whom will be frail and in late old age.

- Direct specific policy attention at the experience of end of life for older adults with dementia and their caregivers.

- Develop an explicit research agenda looking at the situation of older adults facing end of life with no family caregivers.

# 'Places' of care at the end of life

In this chapter, we examine 'places' where older people encounter death and dying, with a view to characterising particular features and experiences of death and dying in different types of setting. We draw some comparisons between the experiences of older people and their family carers where specialist palliative care is accessed and where it is not. We also examine older people's preferences for place of care, drawing both on available research and evidence from the consultation exercise undertaken as part of this review. The former is, however, limited; although death is more common among older people than any other social group, they have only rarely been invited to take part in research about end-of-life care. Similarly, there is little large-scale research on the outcomes associated with different places of care for populations of older people, such as quality of life and costs to service providers.

### The dearth of evidence about best place of care

*The desire to reduce health service costs or improve outcomes for patients is understandable. However it is no more acceptable to develop services based on assumptions about what will achieve these outcomes than it would be to develop clinical interventions on the same basis. If there is a need for evidence based medicine, then there is a need for evidence based services. This review has shown the research agenda required to generate evidence about the best place of care for older people is substantial and also that there is considerable scope for the development of more appropriate primary and secondary methods for such research.*
(Parker et al, 2000, p 189)

As we have seen in the previous chapter, about half of all deaths do not take place in the setting that the dying person prefers; for most, this is at home (Higginson, 2003), although preferences are not necessarily stable and can change over time. While variable patterns of organising services have led to differences in home death rates across the country (Davies and Higginson, 2004a), there is a general trend for the numbers of hospice deaths among older people to decrease as their age increases, while the numbers dying in care homes show a parallel increase. Another important trend relates to moving dying older people immediately before death from their home or care home to hospital. This is indicative of a continued shortfall in the quality of palliative care for many vulnerable older adults living in the community. Most notably, many older adults' experiences of care in the last year of their lives consists of movement between settings as their condition deteriorates. This has been called the 'revolving door' problem (Cartier, 2003) and is marked by 'cost shunting' between health and social services.

## Home care

The provision of services and support at home to all dying people has long been recognised as a goal of healthcare policy. Indeed, the 'good' death is usually characterised as being at home, surrounded by family, friends and familiarity. Dying at home is widely assumed to offer greater autonomy to the dying person and to be less medicalised and more 'natural' than death in any other setting. These assumptions are largely unexamined. However, there is some evidence that the cost of home-based palliative care may be significantly less than inpatient care (Taylor and Carter, 2003). In a discussion about the costs of different models of palliative care delivery, it is noted that the setting in which care is provided at the end of life is "... a key determinant of overall costs" (Whynes, 1997, p 36).

Specialist palliative care services are now designed to predominately support home care at the end of life, working to the principle that admissions to specialist units such as hospices should only be for those patients with distressing symptoms and other complex needs which are not readily relieved in the home and other care settings (NICE, 2004). In the previous chapter, we saw that home deaths were linked to a number of characteristics, including:

- younger age;
- cancer as a cause of death (because of greater access to specialist palliative care services at home);
- being male (because men tend to die younger than women, they are more likely to have a spouse at home to care for them);
- higher socioeconomic status;
- the presence of an informal carer.

Of all of these factors, one of the most important may be the presence of an informal caregiver. A study of community nurses published in 2000 (Addington-Hall and Altman, 2000) reported, for example, that all expressed the view that a home death was 'virtually impossible' if a person was reliant on health and social services and did not have supportive family.

For frail older people who live alone, or with a visiting carer, there has been surprisingly little progress in identifying what is required in order for them to remain at home in spite of their frailty. A key aspect of this is the importance of recognising the need to harness modern technologies in order to make the physical environment of 'home' safer and easier for the older person to live in. Box 3.1 highlights one important project funded by the NHS Estates programme[1], in which it has been demonstrated

---

[1]  Project SHIFT (substitution of hospital in-patient focused technology). Funded by NHS Estates, project reference number B (99) 31, www.nhsestates.gov.uk/download/r_and_d/B_99_31%20Executive%20Summary.pdf (accessed 25 June 2004).

that it is possible to reduce the numbers of older people needing either acute hospital care or requiring admission to care homes, by carefully designed health and social support packages that include assistive technologies.

## Box 3.1: Project SHIFT (substitution of hospital in-patient focused technology)

A review of the problems that affect older people who suffer from the major disabling conditions – heart disease, respiratory disease, dementia and cancer – was followed by the design of three 'bundles' of technology, to assist communication and the activities of daily living and to adapt the environment of care to make it easier for the older person to live safely and in comfort. Predictions were then made about the numbers of people with different degrees of need who could be cared for at home, if these 'bundles' could be made available and what the cost savings would be in terms of hospital care. Among the project predictions was the hypothesis that, among 127 people who were waiting for care admission, 94% of them could have been supported at home if the correct package of care had been available. The authors concluded that:

- High uptake of the single assessment process is of major importance.
- A well-ordered 'just in time' system needs to be developed to replace the poor and reactive system currently in place.
- Equipment maintenance is essential.
- The NHS should provide a capital trust fund and start-up costs.
- The provision must be flexible to accommodate the changing state of frail older people
- Carer training and support is essential.
- Local authorities must reconsider their housing and regeneration policies to include 'smart home' adaptations.
- GPs and community health services need to develop services for frail older people more proactively.

*Source:* Project SHIFT (see Footnote 1)

Some older people who live alone and have chronic life-limiting illness or are extremely frail can also be helped by the provision of direct payments, in lieu of social services provision. Such initiatives can enhance continuity of care and may make care a more rewarding process for all parties. An older man with severe heart disease with whom we consulted reflected on his experience of enhanced continuity and sense of reciprocity:

> "The staff I employ to care for me have become friends: they know exactly what my needs are. I, in my turn, can give something back to them. If I am well enough, I am sometimes able to suggest that we go out for a meal, or I can make some special food for them to enjoy while they are here". (John, living at home with severe heart disease)

Clearly, however, not everyone has the capacity to employ staff in this way and would find the process daunting. Equally, without appropriate adaptations to the home, intermittent input of care will not be adequate in aiding the person to live well at home. John had been ill for many years and had been able, over the course of time to make the adaptations to his home that enabled him to live there in comfort. He wanted us to know that while some people thought he was dying, he was living well in spite of his disabilities and awareness of his limited lifespan.

### Giving care at home to a dying older person: what are the issues?

As we have seen, having carer support is a vital aspect of being able to stay at home for many older people as they face the end of their lives. Box 3.2 summarises bereaved carers' experiences of giving care to dying family members. These findings are typical of a range of research that has emerged over the past 50 years.

Some older people require care over a very long period of time. Exploring the experience of care giving for dementia sufferers, Nolan et al (1996) describe discrete stages in the caregiving experience, including 'taking it on', which typically involves making decisions about treatment and care options without sufficient information or awareness of the

likely implications of these, and 'going through it', in which the skills required to look after an increasingly frail and dependent person are learnt by trial and error. This typology is valuable for helping us to think about the issues involved in giving care to any older person and draws attention to the need for carers to have

---

**Box 3.2: Experiences of giving care at the end of life**

1. A survey of bereaved carers (*n*=301) was conducted to examine satisfaction with services provided for people (the majority of whom were of older age) in the last year of their lives in Powys, Wales, (Ingleton et al, 2004). Deficits were found relating to:

- symptom control;
- nursing care (particularly at night);
- assistance from social services with transport and bathing;
- communication;
- bereavement support.

> "My mother stated all the time until her death [that] she had failed to convince doctor/consultant [about] the pain she was suffering. In my view and I am sure hers, action was taken slowly and of course too late." (Ingleton et al, 2004, p 46)

2. A Canadian study of family members' experiences of caring for a dying person highlights feelings of helplessness, experiences of lack of support and gaps in information and communication (Perrault et al, 2004):

> "Sometimes, I called them up (the nursing agency) and said hurry up! But we had to wait.... I felt uncomfortable ... I saw him suffer and I could not do anything." (p 138)

> "... not having anybody close by that could give you a hand...." (p 138)

> "I gave all I could, honestly ... at the end I could not take it any more ... my strength failed me." (p 139)

opportunities to learn how to care. This was also an important issue to emerge from the consultation exercise undertaken as part of this review (see Box 3.3).

Support programmes for carers of people who have had strokes, providing specific training in basic nursing skills as well as information and emotional support, have been found to improve psychosocial outcomes for both carers and disabled stroke survivors living in the community (Kalra et al, 2004). The attendees at our consultation meeting indicated that such programmes would be valuable, and that it may be possible to develop schemes where bereaved carers, with appropriate help and support, provide support to carers by way of an outreach scheme.

Support for informal caregivers should also be understood as including the period of bereavement or entry to care, when the caregiver must reflect on all that has taken place and try to resume life without the person for whom they cared. This can be a time of significant distress and morbidity, particularly among older adults who are socially isolated.

## Box 3.3: Views expressed at a consultation meeting about caregiving

1. Continuity of care is vital, particularly for people with dementia.
2. Getting help and advice is a fight.
3. Carers can feel that they have let the person down when it is services that are at fault. Feelings of guilt make bereavement worse.
4. Carers take on the role of caring for a dying person with inadequate preparation: they need help learning to care and to cope.
5. Carers could learn from one another: listening to the stories that others have to tell would be helpful.
6. Adapting to life after bereavement when one has been a carer is very difficult: you can feel 'dropped' and isolated.
7. Withdrawal of carers' allowance after the person's death causes financial problems for bereaved carers.

Yet there is evidence that only a minority of people have any opportunity to talk to someone from health or social care agencies at this time. Again, this was something confirmed by those who attended the consultation day conducted in association with this review.

## Older adults' views and experiences of death and dying at home

The meaning of 'home', cultural beliefs about the role of the family, and attitudes towards the different benefits attached to home, hospital, care home and hospice care, influence views about the best place for giving and receiving care during dying. Recent research evidence (Gott et al, 2004), summarised in Box 3.4, suggests that, for a variety of reasons, home deaths are not always viewed favourably by older people, particularly if they fear dying alone or being a burden to others, or if they have concerns about pain, suffering or increasing requirements for intimate bodily care and incontinence.

Home care remains an ideal choice, but not at any price. The concerns that older people have about home care during dying may account for the tendency for reported preferences for home care to decrease as illness progresses. The interview respondents quoted in Box 3.3 were not facing these choices at the time of their interview, although many had past experiences of caring for family members who had died. However, evidence from a study of preferred place of death among people with cancer and their carers, many of whom were older, highlights remarkably similar concerns (Thomas et al, 2004). Similarly, concerns raised about not wanting to be a burden and wishing to remain independent from adult children have been highlighted in studies in other developed countries (Vig and Pearlman, 2003).

## Care homes

'Care home' is a generic term for organisations that offer nursing care and/or personal care depending on their status. Where nursing care is provided, it is funded by primary care trusts. Three levels of nursing care are provided: low, medium and high. The single assessment process is used to determine which 'band' each

## Box 3.4: Older adults' concerns about dying at home

Dying alone
> "I suppose you want your family and friends with you, wherever you are. [It] must be terrible dying alone."

Being a burden
> "I have no daughters, I have just sons and my daughter-in-laws are fantastic but I wouldn't [want to feel] as though I was a burden on them."

Needing intimate care
> "People of this age want their partner with them; they don't want their children there because there's a lot of embarrassing things, and they don't want their sons and daughters attending to them, if you know what I mean. Personal things."

Becoming disabled
> "If he was getting increasing pain and ... [becoming] increasingly physically disabled, like I'm thinking of incontinence and things like that, if he got to that stage, I think he'd be better off in hospital."

Turning home into a hospital
> "I had to make an effort at a time when I didn't want to talk to anybody, I sort of kept going, welcoming everybody and making them coffee and everything at a time when I wanted to shut the door and be on my own.... We reached a stage where this hospice at home took over and they just literally moved in all the equipment that they needed to look after [husband]."

*Source:* Gott et al, 2004, pp 463-5

resident falls into. In 2003, there were 12,944 care homes for older people offering 371,328 beds in the UK. The numbers offering nursing care are falling, while those offering personal care are rising[2]. This is likely to have a significant impact on the experiences of death and dying for residents in care homes.

It has been suggested that a significant number of deaths are hidden from view, or 'sequestered' (Froggatt, 2001) in care homes[3]. Certainly, with a quarter of all older people over the age of 85 years living in care homes, death is a frequent visitor in these settings. Of course, for many older people and their families, entry to care is a positive choice that results in an increase in well-being and a reduction in social isolation, but for some, entry to a care home is involuntary: the result of lack of choice and force of circumstance. For others, a 'temporary' care home stay (perhaps after an episode of acute illness) risks becoming permanent because of the lack, cost and poor coordination of home care services necessary to safely support and help frail adults nearing the end of their lives (Davies and Seymour, 2002). For those who are forced to give up their homes because the cost of care at home is too great or because of a lack of family to care for them, entry to care can be viewed as a forced loss of social roles and social value, with links to family, friends and the local community more difficult to maintain than previously (Davies and Seymour, 2002).

### Patterns of dying and death in care homes

Death in a care home occurs typically after the person has had a gradual deterioration in their overall health over a long period, punctuated by episodes of acute illness. Only about 9% of people who die in care homes do so with a recognisable terminal illness (Siddell et al, 1997). More commonly, death follows a gradual deterioration in the typical 'living on thin ice' pathway to death of the very old (Lynn and Adamson, 2003), as we saw in Chapter 2. Frequently, after death has occurred, it is possible to identify 'critical' events, such as the onset of a chest infection or the reluctance of the person to drink and eat, that pinpoint the beginning of a final stage. One of the major difficulties for residents' families, care home staff and visiting GPs in discussing and making

---

[2]  www.laingbuisson.co.uk (accessed 20 May 2004).

[3]  Froggatt describes sequestration as a social practice that hides away from the public gaze that which is uncomfortable and messy.

appropriate care plans relates to anticipating the meaning and significance of such events as they occur. I lighlighting this, one study of death and dying in care homes reports vividly how some extremely frail older people, who are fully expected to die, survive repeated episodes of acute illness and recover to live with a good quality of life for a number of weeks and months (Froggatt, 2001).

### Older adults' experiences of end-of-life care in care homes

There is comparatively little direct evidence of residents' experiences of end-of-life care in care homes, because of a number of practical and ethical difficulties. A review of available accounts of living in care homes from residents' perspectives suggests that many people experience a loss of personal identity, a sense of isolation, vulnerability and powerlessness, and difficulties in maintaining relationship with friends and family (Davies and Seymour, 2002). In the study of older people's views of end-of-life care drawn on throughout this report (Seymour et al, 2003), this came through vividly in a conversation with 'Leon', a man in his late 80s living in a care home:

> Leon: "I would sooner be at home than here. I've been here too long now, nearly seven year, it's a long time."

> Researcher: "What is it about here that you don't like?"

> Leon: "When they're old people, I don't like old people, me, silly that, isn't it? ... I don't like old people. Can't get on with 'em. I'd sooner be with young people."

> Researcher: "You'd sooner be around young people?"

> Leon: "I would, yeah, any time."

> Researcher: "What is it about the older people here?"

> Leon: "They're all't same I think, it's funny, funny, they don't talk about owt that's sensible. You can't have a conversation with them."

> Researcher: "Right."

> Leon: "You can young 'uns."

> Researcher: "That's why you said earlier about the fact that you like the staff?"

> Leon: "That's right, they're all young 'uns, staff, mostly anyway, very nice people."

In the study by Seymour et al (2003), although some examples of good care were given, bereaved carers tended to portray care homes as engaging in practices that undermined the personhood of older dying people. Accounts of experiences of practices in homes were described in ways that highlighted the problems that can occur when staff and carers have different assumptions about dignity, rights and 'good care'. The provision of food and feeding was perceived to be especially problematic, with references to food and feeding made repeatedly. This is one example:

> "... every six weeks [my husband] went in [to respite care] for two weeks and hated it, he hated it because quite honestly they neglected him, he was neglected.... I went on the Thursday and now, that man hadn't had a wash or a shave from Monday, from Tuesday to Thursday and I just burst into tears and I said but I keep this man immaculate, and to see him – I mean he was, he was partially blind, [and] they brought his food, he couldn't see his food! I went one day and he had food all over his, all over him, and I said I am going to take him home, and that was just one instance." (Seymour et al, 2003)

### Key issues for end-of-life care in care homes

The Care Standards Act (DH, 2000c) implemented in 2000 identifies national minimum standards in choice of home, health and personal care, daily life, social activities, complaints and protection, the environment, staffing and management. These incorporate standards for dying and death (see Appendix D). The presence of other frameworks, such as the National Service Framework for Older People, making slightly different recommendations about end-of-life care (see Appendix B), create complex demands for care home managers and staff.

The delivery of end-of-life care in care home settings is dependent on a range of structural, political, cultural and resource issues that are poorly understood. The following have been identified as particularly important in reports by Froggatt (2001) and Henwood (2001):

- Privatisation of this care sector is widely seen as detracting from quality of care generally. This will have major implications for end-of-life care provision.
- Poorly defined funding for the provision of medical care means that GPs assume such care by default and often reluctantly. Pain management and complex symptom control is sometimes poor as a result, with some evidence of inappropriate medication.
- There is an assumption that a model of palliative care for cancer patients is appropriate for care homes, with a lack of attention to the need to develop models of care informed by gerontology and embedded in the current work of care home staff.
- Residents tend to have complex trajectories of decline and death, with over 50% of deaths attributed to 'general deterioration'. This makes the provision of planned palliative care difficult, and any discussion of residents' preferences problematic.
- While some homes have accreditation as providers of palliative care, most use a pool of untrained care assistants to provide the bulk of care to their residents. These assistants may lack core skills, such as communication and assessment skills, and staff turnover is rapid. Cultural issues may also be important in so far as large numbers of staff may speak English as a second language.
- Relationships between the range of health and social care agencies that intersect with care homes makes care planning very complex, and may lead to conflict in terms of the management of a resident's final illness.
- Care home staff sometimes admit residents to hospital when they are very close to the end of their lives, even though there are fewer admissions to hospital from care homes than from home. This reveals the difficulties care home staff have in managing death well.
- Seventy-five per cent of residents are affected by dementia, and living in environments that are not designed for their care and where staff are not trained to deliver care suitable for their needs. Many adults with dementia endure multiple transitions through the health and social care sectors.
- It has been suggested that care homes are under-funded by between £75 and £85 per person per week. This is likely to have major implications for the quality of end-of-life care that homes can provide.

Confusion and disagreement in relation to the distinction between nursing and personal care have hampered developments aimed at improving and enhancing standards.

**Service provision in care homes**

*The quality of care was rated as needing radical improvement or much improvement in all homes, and no home showed even a fair standard of care.* (Ballard et al, 2001)

*Astonishingly, independent care homes are not viewed as acting as public authorities and are therefore not subject to the Human Rights Act, even where they are providing services under contract to the local authorities.* (Lowe, 2003)

# Hospitals and end-of-life care

As we saw in Chapter 2, most people die in hospital and yet it is widely reported that this in not the place most people want to die (Higginson and Sen-Gupta, 2000; Gott et al, 2004). There is evidence that death in hospital is sometimes poorly managed with inadequate symptom control, poor support for patient and carers and little clear and open communication about prognosis and treatment (Costello, 2001). Older people risk both over- and under-treatment of their disease and symptoms on entry to hospital. Recent initiatives such as the Liverpool Care Pathway (Ellershaw and Wilkinson, 2003) offer a structured approach to ensuring that inappropriate invasive investigations and medical treatments are stopped or not initiated in the final hours or days of life, but they are yet to be fully adopted into practice. We look at this and some other initiatives to improve end-of-life care at the end of this chapter.

A survey of a large general hospital over a five-day period (Gott et al, 2001) sheds some light on the circumstances in which death occurs in hospital settings in the UK. It showed that approximately one quarter of the inpatient population were considered to have palliative care needs by medical and/or nursing staff responsible for their care. Most of these patients were over the age of 60, but age was not seen to be associated with referral to specialist palliative care services and these were predominantly utilised by younger patients. Nurses appeared to be more aware of the palliative care needs of non-cancer patients than were doctors but, overall, the conditions that tend to affect mainly older people, such as strokes and chronic obstructive pulmonary disease, were not seen as requiring palliative care. Doctors and nurses were more able to agree that patients had palliative care needs in cases of cancer, particularly if it was advanced.

Most research about dying in hospital, with some exceptions, presents a gloomy picture of poor quality care in busy, noisy and dirty wards, where medical and nursing staff devote little attention to the dying who are sometimes marginalised in side rooms. Communication with patients and family members is generally inadequate and coordination of services is slow and ineffective (Rogers at al, 2000b). One vivid example of this is a study by Costello (2001), which involved participant observation in a hospital and semi-structured interviews with 74 older patients, 29 nurses and eight physicians. He describes a lack of 'emotional engagement' with the dying older patient and institutionalised practices of non-disclosure of information about death and dying. His observations on acute and continuing care wards led him to conclude that nurses and doctors concentrated on physical care and control of symptoms. While psychosocial, spiritual and emotional care was reported by nurses as important, he found little evidence of nurses being orientated towards this in practice.

## Community hospitals

While the pattern of care for older people dying in larger acute hospitals is bleak, community hospitals offer a more positive alternative. There are 478 community hospitals in the UK,

funded by the NHS and with a median bed size of 26. They are predominantly located in rural areas, staffed by local people and in most GPs can provide continuity of care. Their staff have expertise in the care of older people and, unlike hospices, they are not stigmatised in the public mind as being associated particularly with death. Recent research has indicated that they have the resources, equipment and facilities to care well for dying older people, whatever their diagnosis (Payne at al, 2004). Patients, carers and bereaved carers reported high levels of satisfaction with care received. However, community hospital provision can be limited by competing priorities (rehabilitation versus palliative care), low levels of qualified nursing staff and out-of-hours medical coverage, and a failure to recognise palliative care needs among their older patients until the final stages of dying.

## Older adults' views about dying in hospital

In the study by Seymour et al (2003) of older people's views about end-of-life care, hospitals were seen to provide high-quality technical care, and as such were seen as repositories of specialist care for acute illness and for pain and symptom relief. Echoing the concern sketched out earlier that adult children should not have to deal with overly intimate bodily care, hospitals, and hospices, were seen as a means of containing suffering and dealing with the 'unboundedness' (Lawton, 2000) of the dying person's body:

> "That's when I would want to go in hospital, when I thought I was being too much of a trouble, you know, if you get incontinent and if you get ... well having to wash beds and things everyday ... in our situation we haven't got a dryer, but there's only two of us, we manage all right. But I don't know how we go on if we ... and this would worry me, it would kill me if I were waking up every morning to a problem like that and knowing [my wife] had got to try wash the sheets and things, day after day, no drying weather and things like that."
> (Seymour et al, 2003)

Some participants in Seymour et al's study identified that the drive to keep older people out of hospital care was potentially denying them specialist attention. However, many study participants reported experiences of inadequate 'basic' care provided within the hospital setting, for example in relation to hand feeding and the provision of adequate pain relief and comfort. Hospitals were also reported as invoking 'strangeness' or 'impersonal' care from strangers who are paid to do a job. The threat of being, as one study participant put it, 'just a body', was referred to, the implication being that by being viewed primarily as a body, one's needs for respect and human regard as a person risk being forgotten (Seymour et al, 2003).

### *Does accessing specialist palliative care make a difference?*

There has been an increase in the numbers of hospital-based palliative care teams, which aim to relieve some of these problems. A systematic review (Higginson et al, 2002) indicates that there are modest benefits resulting from these teams but that some standardised outcome measures are needed in order to make more meaningful comparisons. There is evidence that people with terminal cancer are more likely to die where they wish if they are under the care of a multidisciplinary specialist palliative care team (Hearn and Higginson, 1998). They are also likely to spend more time at home and less time in hospital, resulting in a reduction in costs. Most notably, symptom control and patient/carer satisfaction was greater for those under the care of specialist palliative care teams (Hearn and Higginson, 1998).

## Day care

Day care services offer the opportunity for older people to receive services while remaining at home for most of the time. Models of day care provided through specialist palliative care vary from those that are predominantly aimed at medical supervision and nursing care (symptom control, bathing, and so on), rehabilitative and therapeutic (physiotherapy, occupational art, music, drama therapy) or social care (lunch, opportunities to socialise). There is no evidence about which model is most beneficial or appropriate for older people. Patients generally report high levels of satisfaction with day care and carers may benefit from respite. As with

most specialist palliative care services, day care is usually taken up by those with cancer. Day care provision for older adults by other agencies, such as the voluntary sector, could potentially draw on the expertise of the specialist palliative care sector in thinking about how better to support ill and frail clients.

## Initiatives to improve end-of-life care in all settings

While we have not been able to identify any initiatives to improve end-of-life care in the UK that were targeted at older adults per se, lessons can be learnt from:

- The Liverpool Care Pathway (Ellershaw and Wilkinson, 2003): this is a model of care for dying patients developed by the Royal Liverpool University Trust and the Marie Curie Centre in Liverpool. It provides a multi-professional document that gives an evidence-based framework for the management of the dying phase, looking at comfort measures that can be employed, psychological and spiritual support, and communication with the patient, their companions and with the primary healthcare team. The pathway is beginning to be adopted in the UK and elsewhere.

- Gold Standards Framework for community palliative care (Thomas, 2003): this is a framework of standards for both 'in' and 'out of hours' practice, which aims to ensure that people with palliative care needs and their carers have access at all times to the drugs, equipment and well-informed practitioners they need.

- King's Fund programme to support dying people and their carers (King's Fund, 2003): in the past decade, the King's Fund has made 23 grants totalling £459,000 to organisations across London to improve the quality of dying people's final days of life. Projects include support for Rosetta Life's work, which is now a national scheme that helps people to leave behind their life stories, and a befriending network for pairing people with life-threatening illnesses with a volunteer who can provide practical help and companionship. In 1999, the King's Fund conducted a mapping exercise looking at the needs of Londoners who died. Its report, published in 2003, drew attention to the need to stimulate a wider debate about 'good death' and the need to recognise the role of the primary care trusts in providing more integrated care.

- Carer support schemes: during the 1990s, Macmillan Cancer Relief funded seven pilot Carer Support Schemes in England and two in Scotland. These sought to provide practical and emotional help to cancer sufferers and their families living in their own homes. A subsequent evaluation of the schemes showed that they were used predominantly by older people, that they were accessed quickly and that they were associated with high levels of satisfaction by those who used them. The carers provided three main types of help: intimate care (bathing, washing, help with toileting); social and emotional support (listening, talking, providing companionship); and practical help (shopping, cooking and housework) (Clark et al, 2000).

- 'Help the Hospices', a national charity to support hospices, has developed a three-year grant programme to support projects providing hospice or palliative care to people who are terminally ill with diseases other than cancer. The charity is looking to fund small projects that are innovative and that will make a tangible difference to patients' and carers' experiences of death and dying[4].

- The National Council for Palliative Care Services (formerly Hospice and Specialist Palliative Care Services) has, in collaboration with Katherine Froggatt, developed a briefing paper on end-of-life care in these settings (Froggatt, 2004).

---

[4]  www.helpthehospices.org.uk/grants/index.asp
(accessed 12 July 2004)

## Summary and recommendations

This chapter has:

- examined settings of care for older people at the end of life;
- explored older people's preferences for place of care at the end of life;
- drawn comparisons between the experiences of older people who receive specialist palliative care and those who do not.

Key recommendations arising from these discussions include a need to:

- Better understand older people's preferences for place of care at the end of life. This needs to involve a critical examination of the assumption that 'home' is preferred in all instances by reference to the experiences and circumstances of older people facing death. Those factors that support death at home where this is desired need to be better identified. For example, substandard accommodation can make death at home practically difficult. Moreover, many people in late old age do not have relatives or friends available to care for them, yet 'community care' remains fundamentally reliant on the unpaid labours of informal caregivers. While it has been acknowledged that small increases in the amount of home support can make a significant difference to the capacity of frail older adults to remain in their own homes, there remains much to be done in order to mobilise the resources to achieve even these small increases.

- Address the ways in which care for older people who die in acute hospitals and care homes can be improved. It is still the case that the 'good death' is hard to achieve in these settings, because of a complex range of factors including physical environment, the availability of basic equipment and the support and appropriate training of professional staff. Until the care of the dying is afforded a higher priority, many older adults will suffer the experience of either under- or over-treatment at the end of life and will fail to be provided with the good standards of comfort and symptom control that we should all be able to expect. The fact that much of the care of dying older adults lies outside of the NHS is arguably scandalous.

- Recognise the potential for community hospitals to provide good end-of-life care for older adults. It is ironic that in the age of 'intermediate care' some of these locally situated and well-known institutions have been closed or are under threat of closure. Their role as repositories of high-quality general palliative care needs to be recognised and capitalised on.

- Recognise the potential role of day care in providing support for ill and frail older adults facing death. Day care has always played an important role in the provision of hospice care and care of older adults, but there has been little or no liaison between the two models of provision.

# Communication and decision making at the end of life

Communication is a central theme of this report. In this final chapter we look at it in two ways. First, we examine the question of whether or not older people welcome opportunities to discuss death and dying, their views about the 'good' death, and the subjects of bereavement and faith. Faith and religion have been long neglected subjects within research but have great relevance to older adults facing late old age, death or bereavement as they try to make sense of what is happening to them and find meaning in their lives. Second, we look at matters of decision making at the end of life. Here we focus on processes of communication and consultation necessary for planning for the future and what views and experiences older adults have in this area. We look specifically at 'advance care planning' and the issues of consent and autonomy.

## Do older people want to talk?

In thinking about the findings we report here, it is important to remember the enormous heterogeneity of older people. Many of us, of all ages, have difficulties facing the inevitability of our own mortality. However, many older people, who may be worried about the dying process or have practical, existential and emotional concerns related to death and bereavement, have to do this with little or no support.

The few studies (Williams, 1990; Gelo et al, 1997; Howarth, 1998; Field, 2000; Vig et al, 2002; Vig and Pearlman, 2003; Seymour et al, 2003, 2004) that have explored the views of the current older generations about death, dying and end-of-life care indicate that many people are willing to talk about these to researchers,

but that a significant number express reservations or ambivalence. Clearly, there are problems in extrapolating from research to draw conclusions about the role of 'talking' about death and dying in older people's lives, but some useful insights can be gleaned. A brief summary of the main studies follows.

The Mass Observational Study was initiated in 1975 at the University of Sussex and recruits members of the public to write about topics of everyday life. In April 1994, panel members were asked to write about personal experiences of death and bereavement. Fifty-four of these accounts produced by people in the 54- to 80-year age group were selected for analysis by David Field (Field, 2000) at the Centre for Cancer and Palliative Care Studies in London. The panel members are not representative of British society, being predominantly middle-class and well educated. It was noted that several regular correspondents chose not to write about this topic, perhaps because the subject made them feel uncomfortable.

In a study by Glenys Howarth (Howarth, 1998), 72 people over the age of 75 took part in two interviews over a two-year period. The main topic of the study was quality of life. However, during the interviews (and without specific prompting), 58% of the sample raised the subject of death. This ranged from brief mentions of neighbour deaths to lengthy discussions about feelings about their own death and the deaths of close family members.

An interview-based study of attitudes to death and illness among older people living in Aberdeen was conducted by sociologist Rory Williams during the 1980s (Williams, 1990). He did not ask questions directly about death and dying, but most participants raised these issues themselves in their interviews.

Throughout this review, we have drawn on data from a study of 77 older adults' views about end-of-life care (Seymour et al, 2003, 2004). Pictures, story boards and media extracts were used during interviews and focus groups, and the research team was assisted by an advisory group that included participants. Older people from three age cohorts (65-74; 75-84; 85 years and over) and from three contrasting areas of Sheffield, UK took part. They were invited by letter and opted in by returning a card indicating that they were happy for a researcher to telephone them. About one third of those invited took part. Participants were asked debriefing questions at the end of their interview or focus group discussion, and some attended a discussion day at the end of the project where the issue of talking about these subjects was debated. Most reported that they found the use of the third-party stories appropriate and perceived that a more direct technique may have been too invasive. Many stated that they had found participating in the study interesting and enjoyable.

There are a range of North American studies on this topic, although most relate to matters of decision making during serious illness and are not specific to older people. Two small studies (Vig et al, 2002; Vig and Pearlman, 2003) that look specifically at preferences about end-of-life care can, however, be identified. In the first (Vig et al, 2002), 16 non-terminally ill older men and women were interviewed and, in the second (Vig and Pearlman, 2003), 26 older men with a prognosis of less than six months were interviewed. In both studies an introductory 'opt out' letter was sent out via the respondent's physician, asking them to telephone if they did not want to be contacted. It is clear that some people did telephone to decline to participate, although their reasons for so doing are not explored. Additionally, two of the initial interviewees in the first study declined a second interview, saying that the first one had been too depressing and not helpful. In the first study participants were asked a series of open-ended questions, followed by a set of closed questions. Topics covered included their views about a good death, their treatment and care preferences when they were dying, and whether

they would want family, friends and carers with them. The second study used semi-structured interviews to explore what was important to this group of older people as they approached death. Interestingly, these studies say nothing about how the participants felt about talking about end-of-life issues.

The overriding message from these studies is the heterogeneous nature of the responses; assumptions about views and preferences cannot be safely made. Individual exploration of each unique viewpoint is important in supporting older adults at the end of life. Readiness to talk about death and dying is likely to be influenced by personal circumstances. Moreover, facing death, perhaps as a result of terminal or acute severe illness, may well lead to people changing their views and preferences.

## Views about the 'good death'

Age Concern produced a highly publicised framework of the 'good death' in 1999 (see Appendix E). This may be criticised as too ideologically influenced by the rhetoric of the hospice and palliative care movement, in which 'control' and 'choice' (neither readily available to many older people reaching the end of their lives) are paramount. Nor does it reflect the dynamic complexity of views that older people have about this subject, and the way in which these are influenced by cultural attitudes and experiences.

Most of the studies reported here show that older people (and this is likely to be true for all of us) express ambivalent and contradictory attitudes to death and dying. A quick, painless death may be perceived to be 'good' but, equally, a death that gives time for a reunion with family and to settle affairs may be perceived to be preferable. The study by Williams (Williams, 1990) in Aberdeen draws our attention to this. His respondents possessed concepts of 'good' death that were drawn from a variety of cultural and historical influences and were deeply affected by biographical influences:

- Some respondents preferred 'ritual dying', in which achieving readiness for death is combined with an emphasis on the importance of the reunion of the dying with those close to them.

- Other respondents expressed a preference for 'disregarded dying', which combines the moral expectation of death in old age with the ideal of a quick, unaware death.
- A third group of respondents exhibited patterns of 'transitional' ideas about death, in which elements of ritual and disregarded dying are combined.
- A minority group in Williams' study expressed a preference for 'controlled dying', in which the ordering of one's own fate is paramount.

One common feature of all research in this area is that a death that ends pain and long-term suffering is seen as a release; similarly, the control of pain and other symptoms during dying is seen as essential. The terms 'comfort', 'dignity' and 'peacefulness' tend to feature prominently in all accounts of the meaning of 'good death'. How the deaths of others have been experienced is likely to have a profound impact on feelings about this issue and on the course of bereavement. Howarth (1998) found that almost all of her respondents who had witnessed the death of someone close to them were dissatisfied with the way that person had died. One frequent scenario involved the bereaved survivors calling for medical help at home when death was close, which inevitably ended up with admission to hospital. Many spouses regretted this and the fact that the death had occurred in what were felt to be impersonal surroundings with strangers present and medical interventions performed. However, on the other hand, many spoke of the fears they had had of being alone with the person when they died.

## To whom to talk?

It has been suggested that older people perceive that it is essential that they can place their trust in a doctor who knows them well, and that this is a necessary base for discussing matters relating to end-of-life care (Seymour et al, 2002b, 2003, 2004). This desire to trust doctors may be complicated by a lack of clarity about doctors' intentions with regard to end-of-life care or by general ambivalence about speaking with them (Vandrevala et al, 2002). We return to this when we look at decision making. Talking

with family members can also be difficult, with each side trying to protect the other. As a result, while older adults may feel it is important to share their thoughts and wishes about death, dying and end-of-life care with their relatives, this is rarely straightforward:

*"My husband, when ... I am talking about old age and what I want for myself and so on, he turns off the argument, he doesn't want to listen.... I say, 'What do you want for yourself?' and he doesn't want to listen, you know, he ignores it you see."* (Seymour et al, 2004, p 64)

Sometimes, it might be assumed that one's family will not be able to face discussing such subjects when in fact they would welcome the opportunity:

*Mother: "I mean I don't think she'd be very pleased, Fiona, if I sort of said to her, right, come on, we are going to sit down now and I need you to know what I want, what things I want and where I want to be buried and all this, I think she' just get up and walk off!"*

*Fiona (daughter): "I think that it's a good idea actually!"* (Seymour et al, 2004, p 64)

Some families will 'jolly' their older relatives out of any risky discussion, making it difficult for any sustained exploration of important issues to take place:

*"... if I mention death to a couple of my children they oh, granddad, dad, we don't want to hear about that! And the other two make a joke of it, which is what I want; I want them to make a joke of it and be prepared to chat about it."* (Seymour et al, 2004, p 64)

Talking to peers may be an important way in which older people discuss their thoughts and concerns about death and dying. In the studies (Seymour et al, 2002b, 2003, 2004) from which the data presented here are drawn, the older people found participating in discussion groups interesting and enjoyable. Being with a small group of people they knew well was important. This is what one group said at the end of their discussion:

*Heather: "I think perhaps if you look at it from the situation that you hope you're not going to sort of die the next day, the next week or something, I think that bringing things out like we have this morning can probably be very helpful, because it does provide an opportunity to say things that you simply wouldn't have said in any other circumstances. I don't know whether that's what you want us to say? But I think it could...."*

*Harry: "It's been very interesting hasn't it?"*

*Helen: "It's been very interesting ... very good to hear other people's views and experiences."*

*Hilda: "Comfortable."*

*Harry: "We all have different ideas and experience of people dying haven't we? Suffering and that sort of thing, I think it's been very good." (Seymour et al, 2003)*

Attending a faith group or a social group can be a means of obtaining support during illness and bereavement, and may indeed be a route by which thoughts about end-of-life care can be shared and information and experiences exchanged.

Where people find companionship through shared troubles, such as illness or bereavement, this can offer an important opportunity for talk. A participant observation study conducted in a palliative care day centre identified a culture where light-hearted talk about death and dying was apparent among attendees, the majority of whom had life-limiting cancer (Langley-Evans and Payne, 1997). The sample was small (n=14) and the age range wide (mean 59 years), so generalisations are not possible, but it is suggested that talking in this way enabled participants to gain support and help from each other without having to think too much about their own fears. Jokes and humour about death were possible because participants were all in the same situation and were all aware of their prognoses. The authors argue that that humour can be seen as a way of addressing the 'delicate' topic of death while at the same time distancing oneself from the personal implications of it.

Many older adults will have 'inner conversations' about these issues, perhaps relating to their particular spiritual or religious beliefs, or through quiet reflection on literature and other forms of art where the subjects of mortality are addressed. Reading or listening to the stories of other older adults may be preferable to any form of two-way social conversation for some. Thinking about relatives and friends who have died is another important type of 'inner conversation' prevalent in the daily lives of many older adults.

## Attitudes to death and dying

The perceptions of each generation of older adults about death, dying and bereavement are influenced by their different social and cultural experiences. For example, as we mentioned earlier, stoicism in the face of suffering is a traditional stance that many people in late old age are likely to have been brought up to value. This report comes out in the year of the 60th anniversary of D-Day and the memories of the Second World War will inevitably continue to raise vivid images of death for many older men and women.

In studying personal accounts collected by the Mass Observation Archive, Field (2000) was struck by the sheer number of deaths that correspondents describe as having witnessed or been affected by. This is perhaps one reason behind a common finding of the studies examined here in which older people express a general acceptance of death, claiming that they have 'had their day' or 'had a good innings'. One correspondent to the Mass Observation Archive commented:

*"The acceptance that I should die, I shall not in the future exist, is quite different from accepting equably the process of dying, of getting from one state to the other. I hope not to die in a messy or painful or unduly protracted way. But, I don't mind at all the idea of being dead." Female, P1743, aged 65.* (Field, 2000, p 290)

Interestingly, in her study of quality of life, Howarth (1998) notes an acceptance of death among older people with very active social lives, particularly women who cared for grandchildren, neighbours and spouses and who appeared to have a very good quality of life. Clearly, accepting the inevitability of death is not a desire to die, but rather relates to the feeling that one has lived a full life and perhaps lived longer than expected, where each day is the 'icing on the cake'.

## Experiences of bereavement

Many of the older correspondents in Field's (2000) study of the Mass Observation Archive wrote about their memories of people they had lost. Grief and loss featured strongly in their accounts, with many of the cohort still grieving over losses (friends, spouses, parents) many, many years after the death had occurred. Losses accumulate with age. It is not an uncommon experience for one loss to be directly related to subsequent losses, thus complicating and compounding feelings of grief and sadness.

For many older people, particularly older women, growing older will have brought the experience of losing a lifetime partner. This is often associated with parallel changes in lifestyle, income and role. Much research on bereavement has focused on the deaths of younger people and the question has been raised recently as to whether theories that underpin bereavement support are useful for older people. After death, many older people report seeing and, in particular, talking to their dead partner. This is usually reported as a reassuring experience, with the dead person being perceived very much how they had been in life. It is suggested that this maintains a close relationship for some widows/widowers in a situation of loneliness and social isolation. Maintaining contact with a deceased partner through continued conversations, feeling their presence and thinking about them on a daily basis have also been reported (Golsworthy and Coyle, 1999; Costello and Kendrick, 2000). It may be, therefore, that older people retain their relationship with the deceased person in a different way from those who are younger. Given that close relationships that last for 50 or 60 years are not now uncommon, this is not surprising. Psycho-analytical theory about grief work and 'moving on' may be of limited relevance and use for this age group, and there is a danger that uncritical use of traditional models of bereavement will mean that older people may not get the support they need.

## Spirituality, religion and other existential issues

There have been few studies looking at the importance and role of religion, spirituality and faith in older people's lives. Coleman (2001) provides a definition of some of these terms (see Box 4.1).

In the study led by Coleman (Coleman, 2001) (funded by the Economic and Social Research Council as part of its Growing Older Programme), the beliefs of 28, mostly Christian, older people were explored. The study findings show that although there is a tendency to think of Britain as experiencing a decline in religious practice, this does not necessarily correspond to a decline in religious belief. The 28 respondents were categorised as having strong, moderate or weak spiritual beliefs. The relationship between strength of spiritual beliefs and experiences of bereavement was then explored. The findings indicated that strong faith had a positive role in helping people though bereavement. Perhaps surprisingly, having moderate faith (and more so than having a weak faith) was associated with being vulnerable to depression and finding low personal meaning in loss.

Of course, trying to find meaning in the face of death is part of our universal condition, although the contemplation of death is likely to

---

### Box 4.1: Some definitions

Religion: practising a faith in a God or gods, encompassing prayer, ritual and a particular way of life.

Spirituality: concerned with higher levels of meaning and value in life, usually associated with belief in a power or force beyond the material world.

Existential meaning: the belief that 'my' life has meaning and purpose.

*Source:* Based on Coleman, 2001

be discouraged throughout life. For this reason, reflections on mortality in later life may have to be introspective and conducted in isolation, with older people left to deal with their fears and anxieties on their own (Lloyd, 2004). All of these issues need further exploration.

## Whose voices are missing?

Often researchers give little information about their participants. In his comment on the contributors to the Mass Observation Archive, Field (2000, p 279) notes that they are "more likely to come from the upper strata of British society with the lower social classes underrepresented". The population of 'older people' is, as we noted earlier, a varied one, and, although most researchers attempt to take account of socio-demographic factors, recruitment to research projects is often problematic in ensuring even a reasonable degree of representation. Older people from different ethnic groups are often under-represented, as are older people living in care homes or other institutions and older people living in the greatest poverty. We were unable to locate any studies that indicated that the views of older gay men and lesbians were accessed. Additionally, increasing numbers of people with learning disabilities survive to old age (Botsford, 2000), and their perspectives on these issues are also important. Lastly, one hidden and neglected group is that of older people in prison, mainly men, many of whom die in that setting.

## Listening to older people

Cultural stereotyping and perceptions of older people as 'slowing down', 'stupid' or 'dependent' mean that they are less likely to be listened to. Understanding older people's views requires that the people providing services and direct care not only listen to older people, but also support them in expressing their views within a culture that has in the past discouraged or disparaged their opinions. In Chapter 3, we looked at a study by Costello, in which he charted difficulties relating to the care of older people who were dying on a hospital ward (Costello, 2001). This study also highlighted the continuing difficulties with doctor–nurse

communication and how this obstructed any open communication with older patients. Costello's conversations with patients led him to believe that many were just 'working out for themselves' that they were dying. This is a finding seen in other studies (see, for example, the experiences of people with heart failure described in Chapter 2).

> *Failures in communication can cause hardship and distress to patients and their families and carers.... It is clear from the complaints I have received that poor communication both between professionals and with patients remains at the heart of many patients' experience of health care.* (Health Service Ombudsman for England: Annual Report 2002-03, p 17)

Communication has always been a problem in the healthcare professions; 'getting it right' in this sensitive area remains a considerable challenge. It is clear that nurses entering the profession from training feel unprepared for situations that require them to respond to questions and discussions about death and dying (Hopkinson and Hallett, 2002). Dealing with questions from patients and relatives is a source of stress and discomfort, and many nurses will talk about needing emotional detachment, particularly after having upsetting experiences. In one study (Albinsson and Strang, 2002) based on interviews with nurses about how they dealt with topics related to death, dying and meaning raised by dementia patients, nurses reported that they tended to ignore the topic, distract the person, refer to God's control in relation to dying, or respond by showing and giving affection to the older person.

## Anticipating and talking about end-of-life decisions

While most older people remain fit and well into advanced old age, they are likely to have anxieties about the consequences of future life-limiting illness and a heightened awareness of finitude (Munnichs, 1966). These fears may make communication about end-of-life issues a difficult barrier to cross. Some may have concerns about receiving high-technology interventions immediately before death that result in prolonged dying, while others may have fears generated by media 'scandal stories' suggesting that some older persons have been denied the option of life-sustaining treatments (Winterton, 2000). For example, there has been an intermittent debate in the media relating to cardio-pulmonary resuscitation and older people; most famously, in 2000, Age Concern reported the case of a woman with cancer who found that a do-not-resuscitate order had been written in her medical notes without her knowledge (Bates, 2000).

Below, we turn attention to understanding issues relating to decision making at the end of life, examining in particular older adults' perceptions about how critical decisions concerning treatment and care should be made in present time and their ideas about preparing for future incapacity through the device of the advance care statement. We start by setting out some information relating to key elements in this difficult and complex area.

## Some background information

What is the law on 'capacity' and consent?

- There is a legal presumption that adults have the ability (capacity) to make decisions unless this can be proved to be otherwise.
- People have varying levels of capacity at any one time, and decisions that they need to take also vary in their consequences.
- Decisions with grave consequences require a greater degree of capacity.
- Consent must be sought for all medical treatments. To give valid consent people need to be able to access, understand, retain and use information relating to the decision they need to make.
- Information should be provided in simple language and in a variety of modes. All steps should be taken to maximise the decision-making capacity that individuals have.
- Where it is proven that a person lacks capacity, treatment may be provided without their consent where the clinician in charge of their care judges the treatment to be necessary and in that person's best interests. (BMA, 2001)

What do current guidelines say about the involvement of patients and their families in decision making?

- At the time of writing in England, Wales and Northern Ireland (June 2004) no adult can give or withhold consent for the treatment of another adult who lacks decision-making capacity. Just before this report was published, legislation was passed in the form of the 2005 Mental Capacity Act, which allows a designated decision maker to act on behalf of someone who lacks capacity, according to their best interests (summary available at www.dca.gov.uk/menincap/bill-summary.html).
- In Scotland, since 2001 a proxy decision maker can be appointed to give consent for medical treatment for people over the age of 16.
- In determining 'best interests', clinicians must consult with appropriate family members to try to ascertain the person's past wishes, values and preferences. The 2005 Mental Capacity Act gives a legal right to families to be consulted.

What is an advance statement or 'living will?'

- These are statements, given before a person becomes incapacitated, relating to an individual's views and values about their medical treatment. They can be a means of giving advance refusal of particular types of life-prolonging treatments.
- Life-prolonging treatments include cardio-pulmonary resuscitation, artificial feeding and hydration, ventilation and intravenous antibiotics (BMA, 2001).
- A precise definition of advance statements is provided by the British Medical Association (BMA, 1995, pp 3-4):
  - An advance statement (sometimes known as a living will) can be of various types.
  - A requesting statement reflecting an individual's aspirations and preferences....
  - A statement of the general beliefs and aspects of life which an individual values.
  - A statement which names another person who should be consulted at the time a decision has to be made ... the named person's views are not legally binding in England and Wales.

- A clear instruction *refusing* some or all medical procedures (advance directive). Made by a competent adult, this does, in certain circumstances have legal force.
- A statement which, rather than refusing any particular treatment, specifies a degree of irreversible deterioration (such as diagnosis of persistent vegetative state) after which *no* life sustaining treatment should be given. For adults, this can have legal force.
- A combination of the above, including requests, refusals and the nomination of a representative. Those sections expressing clear refusal may have legal force in the case of adult patients.

What does 'euthanasia' mean and is it likely to become legal in the UK?

- There is a wide spectrum of views about euthanasia and there are many misunderstandings about it. It has been defined in the UK as "a deliberate intervention undertaken with the express intention of ending a life to relieve intractable suffering" (House of Lords, 1993-94, p 10). It is illegal in the UK.
- Periodically, there are attempts to change the law. At the time of writing (June 2004) a Bill about assisted dying is under consideration by parliament[1].
- In Belgium and the Netherlands, euthanasia at the voluntary request of a competent adult is now legal under very tightly defined circumstances.
- In the UK, it is now recognised that where death is inevitable, then life-prolonging treatments such as resuscitation, artificial ventilation, dialysis, artificial nutrition and hydration can be withdrawn or withheld, and the goal of medicine redirected to the palliation of symptoms and the provision of 'basic care' and comfort, which must be provided and can never be withheld (BMA, 2001). Basic care includes nursing care, pain relief and relief of other symptoms, the offer of oral nutrition and hydration.

It is acknowledged that giving adequate symptom control or withholding or withdrawing life-prolonging treatments may sometimes

hasten a death that is already expected (BMA, 2001). *This is not euthanasia.*

## *Older adults' experiences of decision making at the end of life*

The current law on decision making at the end of life rests on an assumption that 'autonomy', the right of individuals to be self-determining, is the pre-eminent ethical principle (Seymour and Ingleton, 2004). It is for this reason that, currently, even the person most closely related to you cannot give consent on your behalf if you are unable to express your own view. Individual autonomy can, however, be expressed through the device of an advance statement, as described above. We know very little about whether older adults perceive that 'autonomy' is vitally important in end-of-life decision making or whether in fact, a range of other principles are perceived to be just as important. Here we look at some selected research evidence relating to this.

A valuable study conducted in the Netherlands (Schermer, 2001) followed the cases of 22 hospitalised older people and examined their perspectives on the choices they were faced with at this time. Although the study did not explicitly address end-of-life care, it has much to tell us of relevance:

- Hospital routines meant that the views and values of older people were often not accommodated into decision making, in spite of the well-meaning efforts of individual members of staff. This diminished patients' influence on what happened to them and made it difficult for doctors to think about what was in a patient's best interests.
- There was little evidence of collaborative decision making, in which information is exchanged between doctors and patients during the various phases of decision making. Schermer (2001) identifies five such phases: establishing a relationship; reaching agreement on what the problem and the goals of treatment are; selecting an approach to treatment; deciding which interventions to use; and evaluation and following up.

Some patients preferred to play a passive role in decision making. They preferred to 'entrust'

---

[1] www.publications.parliament.uk/pa/1d200304/1dbills/017/2004017.pdf (accessed 29 June 2004).

their care to doctors. Schermer (2001) argues that we should respect this type of choice and ensure that the trust is enhanced. Ways of achieving this may include training clinicians to listen to patients and express concern and compassion, and paying attention to the organisation of care to ensure relationship continuity.

Some important issues about trust were highlighted in the study of older adults' views about end-of-life care drawn on throughout this report (Seymour, 2002b, 2003, 2004). Many participants had direct experiences of being involved in end-of-life decision making, but understood poorly the clinical, ethical and legal framework within which decisions were made. This was perceived to threaten opportunities for developing the trusting relationships between patients, carers and clinicians identified as a prerequisite of good-quality end-of-life care. Views about the roles of the family and clinical staff in decision making about life-prolonging technologies did not correspond to available guidelines and current law, particularly in relation to participants' beliefs that family should be able to 'veto' particular types of treatment on behalf of older people and, as such, significantly influence the character of the dying trajectory. In spite of this, many participants found it difficult to discuss such issues with their families and had not done so. Addressing these issues through a programme of public education was identified by some participants as an issue that should be addressed urgently if older people and their family carers are to be better equipped to make together informed choices about these aspects of care delivery.

In the consultation exercise undertaken as part of this review, the findings from these two studies (Schermer, 2001; Seymour et al, 2002b, 2003, 2004) were largely validated. Two people spoke of experiences relating to 'do not resuscitate' decisions. In one case, a man reported how his wife (who was very ill with terminal cancer), was asked her views about resuscitation when he had left the room briefly. He felt that the need for such a discussion was not clear and that, if it was required, it should have only taken place when he was there to support his wife. Another person with whom we consulted recalled being asked his views about resuscitation when he was gravely ill and

at risk of dying. Having later recovered, he cast doubt on the idea that one is able to engage with the decision-making process at a time of extreme vulnerability.

### Older adults' views about advance statements

More and more attention is being paid to the potential of the advance statement for enabling patients to express their wishes about treatment. For example, in one hospital trust, an 'expression of wishes in healthcare' form is offered to all older and ill patients asking them to think about treatments in different scenarios of serious illness, such as dementia, stroke or severe physical and mental incapacity (Booth, 2003). We know little about what older people believe and think about such initiatives, or what their information needs are in relation to this.

In the study drawn on at various points in this report (Seymour et al, 2002b, 2003, 2004), the issue of advance statements was explored with focus group participants by means of an extract from the Alzheimer's Society Newsletter and by referring verbally to British Medical Association guidelines (BMA, 1995, 2001). Where participants were able to express beliefs about this issue, they perceived advance statements primarily in terms of their potential to aid personal integrity and to help the families of dying people by reducing the perceived 'burden' of their decision making. They thought it was strange that people planned for their wills or their funerals but did not think much about the care they might want to have at the end of their lives. However, concerns were expressed about the perceived link between advance care statements and euthanasia: some were concerned that completing an advance statement might be interpreted as a request for euthanasia. The term 'pulling the plug' was used by some to describe the sort of clinical actions they thought would follow adherence to an advance care statement. Such concerns and doubts about the meaning of euthanasia and how it differed from permissible forms of non-treatment were raised in relation to all types of care and treatment innovation addressed in the focus groups. Participants also reported worries and difficulties related to thinking about and discussing death and dying, and expressed concerns about the future applicability of advance statements, and the possibility that preferences for care may change (Seymour et al, 2004).

Trust between doctor and patient, built up over time, was perceived to be important in creating an environment in which the communication necessary to underpin advance care planning could take place. Lastly, participants did not perceive that during dying they would be ready necessarily to adhere to an advance statement and 'disengage' from their lives. (Seymour et al, 2004)

We conclude that, rather than emphasising the completion of advance statements, it may be preferable to conceptualise advance care planning as a process of discussion and review between clinicians, patients and families.

Box 4.2 summarises the views, both positive and negative, that people expressed about advance statements.

## Conclusion

Writing in the British Medical Journal, Lesley Fallowfield makes the important observation that:

*Two fundamental issues should be determined when discussing treatment choices with patients – their own preferences about the amount and type of information that is needed and their actual rather than perceived desire for participation in decision making. A clear distinction needs to be made between a desire for information and a wish to assume responsibility for decision making. They are not one and the same thing.... Many studies have shown that patients want much more information than their doctors believe they do. We also know that the ability of doctors to predict which patients want an active, shared, or passive role in decision making is very poor in palliative care and when active, potentially curative treatment is discussed. Patients' preferences about choice of treatment are poorly understood and usually based on intuitive assumptions about their perceived intelligence, age, or quality of life.* (Fallowfield, 2001, p 1144)

It is time that we addressed the points that Fallowfield raises in relation to end-of-life care, to try to improve the experience of dying that all older people and their families have.

---

**Box 4.2: Views about advance statements expressed by focus group participants**

**Positive views**
I want to be asked and this helps me to express my views.
More important than wills.
Family should play a central role.

Helps with control: 'I want to go my way'.

Stops doctors from playing God.

Helps families speak for older people.

**Negative/equivocal views**
I may leave it too late.

I don't want to be asked.
It is difficult to discuss this type of thing with my family.
Family might be too shocked when illness comes and won't remember my instructions.
Does this mean that doctors can commit euthanasia?
You might change your mind and doctors may need to make snap decisions in some cases of sudden illness.

*Source:* Seymour et al (2004)

## Summary and recommendations

This chapter has:

- examined whether older people welcome opportunities to discuss death and dying;
- explored decision making at the end of life, particularly in relation to 'advance care planning', consent and autonomy.

Key recommendations arising from these discussions include the need to:

- Provide education and information for older people on matters of end-of-life decision making, including advance care planning, living wills, euthanasia, consent, and communication; bereavement and loss; and spirituality and faith. Little attention is paid to matters of public education in issues related to end-of-life care, an anomaly in the context of the current emphasis on the importance of choice, autonomy and information.

- Encourage a critical perspective on the idea that choice and control are always the most important factors in good care. While many people wish to play an active part in decision making relating to their treatment and care, some find this daunting, or may prefer to delegate decision-making responsibility to a family member or a clinician. There is a difference between a desire for information and a desire to assume responsibility for decision making. The notion of 'entrusting' one's care to others may be a useful concept to consider in this context.

- Establish that listening to older adults, expressing compassion and concern, and enabling continuity of care through attention to organisational routines are seen as priorities. These are 'basic' tenets of good practice in health and social care, but are neither given the priority they deserve in the training and education of professionals nor nurtured adequately in the pressurised environments of care in which health and social care professionals work.

- Better understand the moral and ethical perspectives that older people regard as important in end of life care, and what are their views about the 'good death'.

- Explore the life stories and spiritual beliefs of older people and how these link to their experiences of the end of life and bereavement.

# Conclusion and recommendations

## Conclusion

In policies relating to older people and to palliative care, quality of life is accepted as the key determinant of decisions relating to care and treatment options; the person and family are understood to be the unit of care, and a strong emphasis is placed on multidisciplinary models of health and social care. Concepts such as 'supportive care', 'rehabilitation', 'dignity', 'respect' and 'autonomy' have become accepted principles of good practice relating to the care of older people in all settings. However, in spite of this rhetoric, ageist stereotypes that predominated in the 20th century, and are only now coming under sustained critique, mean that many older people approaching the last phase of their lives, and their carers, experience systematic and structurally related disadvantage and discrimination.

This report has reviewed evidence relating to this, showing that very old people, who are often women, and those with comorbid states in whom dying is not recognised readily, may be especially at risk. Moreover, although death now almost always occurs at the end of a long life, the issues surrounding death in old age have been obscured from view by a disproportionate emphasis on the more 'heroic' deaths of younger people and by a tendency in gerontological research to neglect death and dying, perhaps because it has been assumed, erroneously, that at the end of life there are few opportunities for individuals to be engaged and involved with the promotion of their own well-being.

We have shown that many older people do wish to engage with these subjects: we need now to find ways in which they can be sensitively involved in consultations about service and education development in this area. The National Council for Palliative Care (2005) has recently identified an urgent need to develop a long-term vision for palliative care: a vision that takes adequate account of the needs of people with advanced, progressive and life-threatening conditions. As we have shown, this means waking up to the fact that such conditions tends to be associated with older age. It is in this context that we offer the following recommendations in the hope that they will make some contribution to the enhanced quality of life of all older people facing death and their families/friends.

## Recommendations

### Practice and education

- Further consultation and dialogue with older people needs to be enabled using a range of modes of engagement, for example through a Citizen's Jury. Regional discussion and consultation groups should be established, with experienced facilitators.
- A programme of information and education about end-of-life care needs to be developed. There has been little emphasis on matters of public education in issues related to end-of-life care, an anomaly in the context of the current emphasis on the importance of choice, autonomy and information. Any public education initiative should include an assessment of older people's preferences for style and should address:
  - information about caring for dying people;
  - matters of end-of-life decision making, including advance care planning, living wills, euthanasia, consent and communication;
  - bereavement and loss;
  - spirituality and faith.

- An oral history archive of older people's stories and experiences of end-of-life care and bereavement should be collected, with a view to making these available for the education, help and support of older people and health and social care professionals.
- Comorbidity and frailty in older age should be recognised as key issues in older adults' experiences of end of life: disease-focused practice is outmoded and leads to socially exclusive practices, poorly integrated care and a lack of forward planning for future needs.
- Developing practical initiatives to help and support frail adults with severe chronic illnesses should take precedence over any concern with defining the 'dying' phase, the basis on which referral to specialist palliative care services and a range of benefits tends to be based currently.
- Consideration should be given to the role of the voluntary sector in end-of-life care for older adults, drawing on the experience of the hospice and palliative care movement. For example, day care (provided in consultation with specialist advisers) may be one way of helping and supporting older adults facing death.
- The development of a carer outreach scheme, using trained peer educators, should be considered. This is something suggested by attendees at a consultation meeting to inform this project.
- Palliative medicine and geriatric medicine should move towards greater coordination, with shared training posts and joint education initiatives.
- Attention should be paid to the potential for assistive technologies to help and support frail older people facing death.
  Education and practice about end-of-life care should encourage a critical perspective on the idea that choice and control are always the most important factors in good care. While many people will wish to play an active part in decision making relating to their treatment and care, some will find this daunting, or may prefer to delegate decision-making responsibility to a family member or a clinician. There is a difference between desire for information and desire to assume responsibility for decision making. The notion of 'entrusting' one's care to others may be a useful concept to consider in this context.

- Listening to older adults, expressing compassion and concern, and enabling continuity of care through attention to organisational routines should be seen as priorities. These are 'basic' tenets of good practice in health and social care, but are neither given the priority they deserve in the training and education of professionals nor nurtured adequately in the pressurised environments of care in which health and social care professionals work.

## Policy

- Recognising better end-of-life care for older adults is an urgent public health issue, in keeping with the stance of the World Health Organization on palliative care. A helpful step would be to map out the variety of service provision, resources and models of care that are relevant to the end-of-life care of older adults, and to facilitate dialogue about how best to mobilise scarce resources in pursuit of better end-of-life care for us all.
- There is an urgent need for a cross-agency collaborative to address the issues of end-of-life care for older adults. It is encouraging to note the gradual emergence of this issue onto the agenda of a range of contributors to policy making. There is an opportunity for these agencies to lead the way in demonstrating how collaboration, communication and cross-agency working can be facilitated, and to work towards the implementation of practical solutions to address what are fundamental inadequacies in end-of-life care for older adults.
- A critical and realistic debate should be opened with regard to the possible role of specialist palliative care in the care of older people. The links between specialist palliative care providers and the voluntary sector, and between specialist palliative care providers, primary and geriatric care, should be examined.
- The implications for end-of-life care in all policy recommendations for older adults need to be scrutinised. There is currently a profound lack of consideration of such issues across the policy spectrum.
- Attention should be paid to efforts to develop models of user engagement with people facing death: ongoing work at the

universities of Sheffield and Lancaster and funded by Macmillan Cancer Relief and St Christopher's Hospice is of direct relevance here.

- Specific policy attention should be directed to the end-of-life experiences of older adults who live alone, many of whom are frail, in late old age and lack readily available carers.
- The intersection between poverty in older age and the quality of environment and care that older adults encounter at the end of life requires close scrutiny: the specialist palliative care movement has largely ignored the material and economic influences on dying, and yet these critically shape older adults' access to the care resources that can enable 'good death'.
- Specific policy attention should be directed to the end-of-life experiences of older adults with dementia and their caregivers.
- There is a need to address the ways in which care for older people who die in acute hospitals and care homes can be improved. It is still the case that the 'good death' is hard to achieve in these settings, because of a complex range of factors including their physical environment, lack of availability of basic equipment and the lack of support and appropriate training of professional staff. Until the care of the dying is afforded higher priority, many older adults will suffer the experience of either under- or over-treatment at the end of life and will fail to be provided with the good standards of comfort and symptom control that we should all be able to expect. The fact that much of the care of dying older adults lies outside of the NHS is arguably scandalous.
- The idea that 'home' is best should be critically examined by reference to the experiences and circumstances of older people facing death. Those factors that support death at home where this is desired need to be better identified. For example, substandard accommodation can make death at home difficult in practice. Moreover, many people in late old age do not have relatives or friends available to care for them, yet 'community care' remains fundamentally reliant on the unpaid labours of informal caregivers. While it has been acknowledged that small increases in the amount of home support can make a significant difference to the capacity of frail older adults to remain in

their own homes, there remains much to be done in order to mobilise the resources to achieve even these small increases.

## Research

- We need to better understand the experience of end of life for older adults living alone, in late old age and with dementia.
- There needs to be an explicit research agenda looking at the situation of older adults facing end of life with no family caregivers.
- We need to better understand the moral and ethical perspectives that older people regard as important in end-of-life care, and their views about the 'good death'.
- We need to better understand the life stories and spiritual beliefs of older people and how these link to their experiences of the end of life and bereavement.
- We need to better understand diversity and cultural issues in end-of-life care for older people.

# References

Addington-Hall, J.M. (1998) *Reaching out: Specialist palliative care for adults with non-malignant disease*, London: NCHSPCS.

Addington-Hall, J.M. and Altman, D. (2000) 'Which terminally ill patients in the United Kingdom receive care from community specialist palliative care nurses?', *Journal of Advanced Nursing*, vol 32, no 4, pp 799-806.

Addington-Hall, J.M. and McCarthy, M. (1995) 'Regional study of care for the dying: methods and sample characteristics', *Palliative Medicine*, vol 9, pp 27-35.

Addington-Hall, J.M, Fakhoury, W. and McCarthy, M. (1998) 'Specialist palliative care in non-malignant disease', *Palliative Medicine*, vol 12, pp 417-27.

Albinsson, L. and Strang, P. (2002) 'A palliative approach to existential issues and death in end-stage dementia care', *Journal of Palliative Care*, vol 18, no 3, pp 168-74.

Aldred, H., Gott, M. and Gariballa, S. (2005) 'A qualitative study to explore the impact of advanced heart failure on the lives of older patients and their informal carers', *Journal of Advanced Nursing*, vol 49, no 2, pp 116-24.

Alzheimer's Disease International (1999) 'Fact sheet 4: the demography of ageing around the world', www.alz.co.uk (accessed 14 May 2004).

Alzheimer's Society (2000) *Food for thought*, London: Alzheimer's Society.

Anderson, K. and Dimond, M. (1995) 'The experience of bereavement in older adults', *Journal of Advanced Nursing*, vol 22, no 2, pp 308-15.

Ballard, C., Fossey, J., Chithramohan, R., Howard, R., Burns, A., Thompson, P., Tadros, G. and Fairbairn, A. (2001) 'Quality of care in private sector and NHS facilities for people with dementia: cross sectional survey', *BMJ*, vol 323, no 7310, pp 426-7.

Bates, L. (2000) 'Cancer patient's fury at doctor who "wrote her off on hospital's death ward"', *The Guardian*, 13 April.

Blackhall, L.J., Frank, G., Murphy, S.T., Michel, V., Palmer, J.M. and Azen, S.P. (1999) 'Ethnicity and attitudes towards life sustaining technology', *Social Science and Medicine*, vol 48, no 12, pp 1779-89.

BMA (British Medical Association) (1995) *Advance statements about medical treatment*, London: BMA.

BMA (2001) *Withholding and withdrawing life-prolonging medical treatment*, London: BMA.

Booth, J. (2003) 'Hospital gives elderly the chance to choose how and when they die', *The Sunday Telegraph*, 23 February, p 10.

Botsford, A. (2000) 'Integrating end of life care into services for people with an intellectual disability', *Social Work Health Care*, vol 31, no 1, pp 35-48.

Bury, M. and Holme, A. (1991) *Life after ninety*, London: Routledge.

Cartier, C. (2003) 'From home to hospital and back again: economic restructuring, end of life, and the gendered problems of place-switching health services', *Social Science and Medicine*, vol 56, no 11, pp 2289-301.

Cartwright, A. (1993) 'Dying when you're old', *Age and Ageing*, vol 22, pp 425-30.

Cartwright, A., Hockey, L. and Anderson, J.L. (1973) *Life before death*, London: Routledge and Kegan Paul.

Clark, D., Ferguson, C. and Nelson, C. (2000) 'Macmillan Carers' Schemes in England: results of a multi centre evaluation', *Palliative Medicine*, vol 14, pp 129-39.

Cohen-Mansfield, J., Rabinovich, B.A., Lipson, A., Fein, A., Gerber, B., Weissman, S. and Pawlson, L.G. (1991) 'The decision to execute a durable power of attorney for health care and preferences for life sustaining treatments in nursing home residents', *Archives of Internal Medicine*, vol 151, no 2, pp 289-94.

Coleman, P. (2001) *Spiritual beliefs and existential meaning in later life*, Growing older programme newsletter no 2, Economic and Social Research Council (www.shef.ac.uk/uni/projects/newslet2.pdf).

Costello, J. (2001) 'Nursing older dying patients: findings from an ethnographic study of death and dying in elderly care wards', *Journal of Advanced Nursing*, vol 35, no 1, pp 59-68.

Costello, J. and Kendrick, K. (2000) 'Grief and older people: the making or breaking of emotional bonds following partner loss in later life', *Journal of Advanced Nursing*, vol 32, no 6, pp 1374-82.

Cox, S. and Cook, A. (2002) 'Caring for people with dementia at the end of life', in J. Hockley and D. Clark (eds) *Palliative care for older people in care homes*, Buckingham: Open University Press, pp 86-103.

Davies, E. and Higginson, I. (eds) (2004a) *Better palliative care for older people*, Copenhagen: World Health Organization Europe.

Davies, E. and Higginson, I. (eds) (2004b) *The solid facts: Palliative care*, Copenhagen: World Health Organization Europe.

Davies, S. and Seymour, J. (2002) 'Historical and policy contexts', in J. Hockley and D. Clark (eds) *Palliative care for older people in care homes*, Buckingham, Open University Press.

Debate of the Age Health and Care Study Group (1999) *The future of health and care of older people: The best is yet to come*, The Millennium Papers, London: Age Concern.

DH (Department of Health) (1987) HC(87)4(2), London: DH.

DH (2000a) *The NHS cancer plan: A plan for investment, a plan for reform*, London: The Stationery Office.

DH (2000b) *National Service Framework for coronary heart disease: Modern standards and service models*, London: The Stationery Office.

DH (2000c) *Care homes for older people. National minimum standards. Care Standards Act 2000*, London: The Stationery Office.

DH (2001) *The National Service Framework for Older People*, London: The Stationery Office.

DH (2002) *Care homes for older people. National minimum standards*, London: The Stationery Office.

DH (2003) *Discharge from hospital: Pathway, progress and practice*, London: The Stationery Office.

DH (2004) *All our lives: Social care in England 2002-2003*, London: The Stationery Office.

DWP (Department for Work and Pensions) (2002) *Pension Analysts' Division: Pensioners' income series 2000/01, Section 9* (www.dwp.gov.uk) (accessed 18 June 2004).

Ellershaw, J. and Wilkinson, S. (eds) (2003) *A pathway to excellence*, Oxford: Oxford University Press.

Expert Advisory Group on Cancer [The Calman-Hine Report] (1995) *A policy framework for commissioning cancer services: A report by the Expert Advisory Group on Cancer to the Chief Medical Officers of England and Wales*, London: DH/Welsh Office.

Fallowfield, L. (2001) 'Participation of patients in decisions about treatment for cancer', *BMJ*, vol 323, no 7322, p 1144.

Field, D. (2000) 'Older people's attitudes towards death in England', *Mortality*, vol 5, no 3, pp 277-97.

Forbes, S., Bern-Klug, M. and Gessert, C. (2000) 'End-of-life decision making for nursing home residents with dementia', *Journal of Nursing Scholarship*, vol 32, no 3, pp 251-8.

Froggatt, K. (2001) 'Life and death in English nursing homes: sequestration or transition? ', *Ageing and Society*, vol 21, no 3, pp 319-32.

Froggatt, K. (2004) *Palliative care in care homes for older people*, National Council for Palliative Care.

Gelo, F., O'Brien, L. and O'Connor, B. (1997) 'Nursing home residents' perception of the good death', *Journal of Religious Gerontology*, vol 10, no 2, pp 19-27.

Gillick, M.R. (2000) 'Rethinking the role of tube feeding in patients with advanced dementia', *The New England Journal of Medicine*, vol 342, no 3, pp 206-9.

GMC (General Medical Council) (2002) *Withdrawing and withholding life prolonging treatments: Good practice in decision making*, Guidance from the Standards Committee of the General Medical Council, London: GMC.

Golsworthy, R. and Coyle, A. (1999) 'Spiritual beliefs and the search for meaning among older adults following partner loss', *Mortality*, vol 4, no 1, pp 21-40.

Gott, M., Ahmedzai, S.H. and Wood, C. (2001) 'How many inpatients at an acute hospital have palliative care needs? Comparing the perspectives of medical and nursing staff', *Palliative Medicine*, vol 15, no 6, pp 451-60.

Gott, M., Seymour, J.E., Bellamy, G., Clark, D. and Ahmedzai, S.H. (2004) 'Older people's views about home as a place of care at the end of life', *Palliative Medicine*, vol 18, pp 460-7.

Grande, G.E., Addington- Hall, J.M., et al (1998) 'Place of death and access to home care services: are certain patient groups at a disadvantage? ', *Social Science and Medicine*, vol 47, no 5, pp 565-78.

Griffin, J. (1991) *Dying with dignity*, London: Office of Health Economics.

Hawley, C. (2003) 'Is it ever enough to die of old age?', *Age and Ageing*, vol 32, no 5, pp 484-6.

Health Service Ombudsman for England (2003) Annual Report 2002-03. Fourth report-session 2002-03, London: The Stationery Office.

Hearn, J. and Higginson, I.J. (1998) 'Do specialist palliative care teams improve outcomes for cancer patients? A systematic literature review', *Palliative Medicine*, vol 15, no 5, pp 317-32.

Help the Aged (2002) *Making decisions around the end of life*, Policy statement, London: Help the Aged.

Help the Aged (2003) *Cold homes: The UK's winter death scandal*, Policy statement, London: Help the Aged.

Henwood, M. (2001) *Future imperfect? Report of the King's Fund care and support inquiry*, London: King's Fund.

Higginson, I.J. (1997) *Palliative and terminal care: Health care needs assessment: The epidemiologically based needs assessment reviews*, Oxford: Radcliffe Medical Press.

Higginson, I.J. (2003) *Priorities and preferences for end of life care in England, Wales and Scotland*, London: NCHSPCS.

Higginson, I.J. and Sen-Gupta, G.J.A. (2000) 'Place of care in advanced cancer: a qualitative systematic literature review of patient preferences', *Journal of Palliative Care*, vol 3, pp 287-300.

Higginson, I.J., Astin, P. and Dolan, S. (1998) 'Where do cancer patients die? Ten-year trends in the place of death of cancer patients in England', *Palliative Medicine*, vol 12, pp 353-63.

Higginson, I.J., Finlay, I., Goodwin, G.M., Cook, A.M., Hood, K., Edwards, A.G.K., Douglas, H.R. and Norman, C.E. (2002) 'Do hospital-based palliative teams improve care for patients or families at the end of life?', *Journal of Pain and Symptom Management*, vol 23, no 2, pp 96-106.

Hofman, A., Rocca, W.A., Brayne, C., Breteler, M.M., Clarke, M., Cooper, B., Copeland, J.R., Dartigues, J.F., da Silva Droux, A., Hagnell, O. (1991) 'The prevalence of dementia in Europe: a collaborative study of 1980-1990', *International Journal of Epidemiology*, vol 20, pp 736-48.

Hopkinson, J.A. and Hallet, C. (2002) 'Good death? An exploration of newly qualified nurses' understanding of good death', *International Journal of Palliative Nursing*, vol 8, no 11, pp 532-9.

Horne, G. and Payne, S. (2004) 'Removing the boundaries: palliative care for patients with heart failure', *Palliative Medicine*, vol 18, no 4, pp 291-6.

House of Lords (1993-94) *Report of the Select Committee on Medical Ethics*, HL Paper 21-I, London: The Stationery Office.

Howarth, G. (1998) 'Just live for today: living, caring, ageing, dying', *Ageing and Society*, vol 18, no 6, pp 673-89.

Hoyland, J. (1997) 'Thanks NHS, for a rotten way to die', *Independent Tabloid*, 22 April, pp 8-9.

Ingleton, C., Morgan, J., Hughes, P., Noble, B., Evans, A. and Clark, D. (2004) 'Carer satisfaction with end of life care in Powys, Wales: a cross-sectional survey', *Health and Social Care in the Community*, vol 12, no 1, pp 43-52.

Jones, A.M., O'Connell, J.E. and Gray, S.C. (2003) 'Living and dying with congestive heart failure: addressing the needs of older congestive heart failure patients', *Age and Ageing*, vol 32, no 6, pp 566-8.

Joy, I. and Standford, S. (2004) *Caring about dying*, London: New Philanthropy Capital.

Kafetz, K. (2003) 'What happens when elderly people die?', *Journal of the Royal Society of Medicine*, vol 95, no 11, pp 536-8.

Kalra, L., Evans, A. and Perez, I. (2004) 'Training caregivers of stroke patients: randomized controlled trial', *BMJ*, vol 328, no 7448, pp 1099-2004.

King's Fund (1999) *When we are very old: Reflections on treatment, care and support of older people*, London: King's Fund Publishing.

King's Fund (2003) *Supporting dying people and their carers: The King's Fund Role and Work*, www.kingsfund.org.uk/pdf/SupportingDying People.pdf (accessed 12 July 2004).

Klinkenberg, M. (2003) *The last phase of life of older people: Health, preferences and care. A proxy report study*, PhD thesis, The Netherlands: Institute for Research in Extramural Medicine, Vrije University Medical Centre.

Kovach, C.R., Weissman, D.E., Griffe, J., Matson, S. and Muchka, S. (1999) 'Assessment and treatment of discomfort for people in late-stage dementia', *Journal of Pain and Symptom Management*, vol 18, no 6, pp 412-19.

Langley-Evans, A. and Payne, S. (1997) 'Light-hearted death talk in a palliative day care context', *Journal of Advanced Nursing*, vol 26, no 6, pp 1091-7.

Lawton, J. (2000) *The dying process: Patients' experiences of palliative care*, London: Routledge.

Levenson, J.W., McCarthy, E.P., Lynn, J., Davis, R.B. and Phillips, R.S. (2000) 'The last six months of life for patients with congestive heart failure', *Journal of American Geriatric Society*, vol 48, Supplement, pp 101-9.

Lloyd, L. (2004) 'Morality and mortality: ageing and the ethics of care', *Ageing and Society*, vol 24, no 2, pp 235-6.

Lloyd-Williams, M. and Payne, S. (2002) 'Can multi-disciplinary guidelines improve the palliation of symptoms in the terminal phase of dementia', *International Journal of Palliative Nursing*, vol 8, no 8, pp 370-5.

Lowe, S. (2003) 'In need of an anchor' (www.communitycare.co.uk/article) (accessed 9 July 2004).

Lynn, J. and Adamson, D.M. (2003) *Living well to the end of life: Adapting health care to serious chronic illness in old age*, Arlington, VA: Rand Health.

Lynn, J., Teno, J.M., Phillips, R.S., Wu, A.W., Desbiens, N., Harrold, J., Claessens, M.T., Wenger, N., Kreling, B. and Connors Jr., A.F. (1997) 'Perceptions by family members of the dying experience of older and seriously ill patients', *Annals of Internal Medicine*, vol 126, no 2, pp 97-106.

Macdonald, A., Carpenter, G.I., Box, O., Roberts, A. and Sahu, S. (2002) 'Dementia and the use of psychotropic medication in non "elderly mentally infirm" nursing homes in South East England', *Age and Ageing*, vol 31, no 1, pp 58-64.

Marie Curie Memorial Foundation and the Queen's Institute of District Nursing (1952) *Report on a national survey concerning people with cancer nursed at home*, London: Marie Curie Memorial Foundation.

McCarthy, M., Ley, M. and Addington-Hall, J.M. (1996) 'Dying from heart disease', *Journal of Royal College of Physicians*, vol 30, no 4, pp 325-8.

McCarthy, M., Addington-Hall, J.M. and Altmann, D. (1997a) 'The experience of dying with dementia: a retrospective study', *International Journal of Geriatric Psychiatry*, vol 12, no 3, pp 404-9.

McCarthy, M., Addington-Hall, J.M. and Ley, M. (1997b) 'Communication and choice in dying from heart disease', *Journal of the Royal Society of Medicine*, vol 90, no 3, pp 128-31.

McInerney, F. (1992) 'Provision of food and fluids in terminal care: a sociological analysis', *Social Science and Medicine*, vol 34, no 11, pp 1271-6.

Meier, D.E., Ahronheim, J.C., Morris, J., Baskin-Lyons, S. and Morrison, R.S. (2001) 'High short-term mortality in hospitalised patients with advanced dementia: lack of benefit of tube feeding, *Archives of Internal Medicine*, vol 161, no 4, pp 594-9.

Munnichs, J. (1966) *Old age and finitude*, New York, NY: Karger.

Murray, S.A., Boyd, K., Kendall, M., Worth, A., Benton, T.F. and Clausen, H. (2002) Dying of lung cancer or cardiac failure: prospective study of patients and their carers in the community, *BMJ*, vol 325, no 7370, p 929.

National Council for Palliative Care (2005) *20:20 vision*, London: National Council for Palliative Care.

National Statistics (2003) *Mortality statistics: General. Review of the Registrar General on deaths in England and Wales, 2001. Series DH1 no. 34*, London: Office for National Statistics.

National Statistics (2004) *Living in Britain: Results from the 2002 General Household Survey: No 31*, London: The Stationery Office.

National Statistics Online (2004) 'Focus on older people, www.statistics.gov.uk/focuson/olderpeople (accessed 21 May 2004).

NCHSPCS (National Council for Hospice and Specialist Palliative Care Services) (1995) *Specialist palliative care: A statement of definitions*, London: NCHSPCS.

NCHSPCS (1999) *The Palliative Care Survey 1999*, London: NCHSPCS.

NCHSPCS (2002) *Definitions of supportive and palliative care*, London: NCHSPCS.

NICE (National Institute for Clinical Excellence) (2004) *Improving supportive and palliative care for adults with cancer*, London: NICE.

Nolan, M., Grant, G. and Keady, J. (1996) *Understanding family care*, Buckingham: Open University Press.

Office of the Deputy Prime Minister (1998) *English House Condition Survey*, London: The Stationery Office.

Parker, G., Bhakta, P., Katbamna, S., Lovett, C., Paisley, S., Parker, S., Phelps, K., Baker, R., Jagger, C., Lindesay, J., Shepperdson, B. and Wilson, A. (2000) 'Best place of care for older people after acute and during subacute illness: a systematic review', *Journal of Health Services Research and Policy*, vol 5, no 3, pp 176-98.

Payne, S., Kerr, C., Hawker, S., Seamark, D., Davis, C., Roberts, H., Jarrett, N., Roderick, P. and Smith, H. (2004) 'A survey of the provision of palliative care in community hospitals: an unrecognised resource', *Journal of the Royal Society of Medicine*, vol 97, no 9, pp 428-31.

Peck, A., Cohen, C.E. and Mulvihill, M.N. (1990) 'Long-term enteral feeding of aged demented nursing home patients', *Journal of the American Geriatric Society*, vol 38, no 11, pp 1195-8.

Perrault, A., Fothergill-Bourbannais, F. and Fiset, V. (2004) 'The experience of family members caring for a dying loved one', *International Journal of Palliative Nursing*, vol 10, no 3, pp 133-43.

Rogers, A., Addington-Hall, J.M., Abery, A., McCoy, A.S.M., Bulpitt, C., Coats, A.J.S. and Gibbs, J.S.R. (2000a) 'Knowledge and communication difficulties for patients with chronic heart failure: qualitative study', *BMJ*, vol 321, no 7261, pp 605-7.

Rogers, A., Karlsen, S. and Addington-Hall, J.M. (2000b) '"All the services were excellent. It is when the human element comes in that things go wrong": dissatisfaction with hospital care in the last year of life', *Journal of Advanced Nursing*, vol 3, no 4, pp 768-74.

Ross, M. and Fisher, R. (2000) *A guide to end-of-life care for seniors*, Ottawa: Health Canada.

Royal Commission on Long-Term Care (1999) *With respect to age: Long-term care, rights and responsibilities*, London: The Stationery Office.

Saunders, C. and Baines, M. (1983) *Living with dying: The management of terminal illness*, Oxford: Oxford University Press.

Schermer, M. (2001) *The different faces of autonomy: A study on patient autonomy in ethical theory and hospital practice*, Amsterdam: University of Amsterdam.

Seale, C. and Cartwright, A. (1994) *The year before death*, Aldershot: Avebury.

Secretary of State for Health (1999) *Saving lives: Our healthier nation*, CM 4386, London: The Stationery Office.

Sepulveda, C., Marlin, A., Yoshida, T. and Ullrich, A. (2002) 'Palliative care: the World Health Organization's global perspective', *Journal of Pain and Symptom Management*, vol 24, no 2, pp 91-6.

Seymour, J.E. (2002) 'Artificial feeding at the end of life: older people's understandings', in C. Gastmans (ed) *Between technology and humanity: The impact of new technologies on health care ethics*, Brussels: Leuven University Press.

Seymour, J.E. and Hanson, E. (2000) 'Palliative care and older people', in M. Nolan, S. Davies and G. Grant (eds) *Working with older people and their families*, Buckingham: Open University Press.

Seymour, J.E. and Ingleton, C. (2004) 'Transitions into the terminal phase', in S. Payne, J.E. Seymour and C. Ingleton (eds) (2004) *Palliative care nursing: Principles and evidence for practice*, Buckingham: Open University Press, pp 189-217.

Seymour, J.E., Clark, D. and Marples, R. (2002a) 'Palliative care and policy in England: a review of health improvement plans for 1999-2003', *Palliative Medicine*, vol 16, pp 5-11.

Seymour, J.E., Clark, D., Gott, M., Bellamy, G. and Ahmedzai, S.H. (2002b) 'Good deaths, bad deaths: older people's assessments of risks and benefits in the use of morphine and terminal sedation in end of life care', *Health, Risk and Society*, vol 4, no 3, pp 287-303.

Seymour, J.E., Gott, M., Clark, D. and Ahmedzai, S.H. (2003) *Technology and natural death: A study of older people*, Report to the Economic and Social Research Council (www.regard.ac.uk).

Seymour J.E., Gott, M., Bellamy, G., Clark, D. and Ahmedzai, S.H. (2004) 'Planning for the end of life: the views of older people about advance care statements', *Social Science and Medicine*, vol 59, no 1, pp 57-68.

Siddell, M., Katz, J. and Komaromy, C. (1997) *Death and dying in residential and nursing homes for older people: Examining the case for palliative care*, Report for the Department of Health, Milton Keynes: Open University.

Skilbeck, J., Mott, L., Smith, D., Page, H. and Clark, D. (1997) 'Nursing care for people dying of chronic obstructive airways disease', *International Journal of Palliative Care Nursing*, vol 3, no 2, pp 100-6.

SMAC (Standing Medical Advisory Committee)/ SNMAC (Standing Nursing and Midwifery Advisory Committee) (1992) *The principles and provision of palliative care*, London: HMSO.

Social Services Inspectorate (2003) *Improving older people's services: An overview of performance*, London: Social Services Inspectorate.

Tallis, R. (1999) 'Old faces, new lives', *Times Higher Educational Supplement*, 9 July.

Taylor, D. and Carter, S. (2003) 'Valuing choice – dying at home. A case for the more equitable provision of high quality support for people who wish to die at home', unpublished report to Marie Curie Cancer Care.

Thomas, C., Morris, S.M. and Clark, D. (2004) 'Place of death: preferences among cancer patients and their carers', *Social Science and Medicine*, vol 58, no 12, pp 2431-44.

Thomas, K. (2003) 'The Gold Standards Framework in community palliative care', *European Journal of Palliative Care*, vol 10, no 3, pp 1143-45.

Van der Steen, J., Ooms, M., van der Wal, G., Ribbe, M.W. (2002) 'Pneumonia: the demented patient's best friend? Discomfort after starting or withholding antibiotic treatment', *Journal of the American Geriatrics Society*, vol 50, no 10, pp 1681-8.

Vandrevala, T., Hampson, S.E. and Chrysanthaki, T. (2002) 'Breaking the death taboo: older people's perspectives on end-of-life decisions', *Quality in Ageing-Policy, Practice, and Research*, vol 3, no 3, pp 36-43.

Vig, E.K. and Pearlman, R.A. (2003) 'Quality of life while dying: a qualitative study of terminally ill older men', *Journal of American Geriatric Society*, vol 51, no 11, pp 1595-601.

Vig, E., Davenport, N.A. and Pearlman, R.A (2002) 'Good deaths, bad deaths and preferences for the end of life: a qualitative study of geriatric outpatients', *Journal of American Geriatric Society*, vol 50, no 9, pp 1541-51.

Ward, C. (2002) 'The need for palliative care in the management of heart failure', *Heart* (British Cardiac Society), vol 87, no 3, pp 294-8.

Wasson, K., Tate, H. and Hayes, C. (2001) 'Food refusal and dysphagia in older people with dementia: ethical and practical issues', *International Journal of Palliative Nursing*, vol 7, no 10, pp 465-71.

Whynes, D. (1997) 'Costs of palliative care', in D. Clark, J. Hockley and S. Ahmedzai (eds) *New themes in palliative care*, Buckingham: Open University Press.

Williams, R. (1990) *The Protestant legacy: Attitudes to death and illness among older Aberdonians*, Oxford: Clarendon Press.

Winter, S.M. (2000) 'Terminal nutrition: framing the debate for the withdrawal of nutritional support in terminally ill patients', *American Journal of Medicine*, vol 109, no 9, pp 723-6.

Winterton, A. (2000) 'We must stop murdering the old and infirm', *Daily Telegraph*, 27 January.

Woolhead, G., Calnan, M., Dieppe, P. and Tadd, W. (2004) 'Dignity in older age: what do older people in the United Kingdom think?', *Age and Ageing*, vol 33, no 2, pp 165-70.

Working Group on Terminal Care [The Wilkes Report] (1980) *Report of the Working Group on Terminal Care*, London: Department of Health and Social Security.

Young, M. and Cullen, L. (1996) *A good death. Conversations with East Londoners*, London: Routledge.

# Appendix A: Articles on death and dying written by older people

## 1   Jean M. Buzan

You ask how I feel [aged nearly 88], knowing I am definitely in the final years of my relatively long life – do I think about it, talk about it, worry about it?

The reply to the first two is a definite affirmative. Yes, I do think about it quite a lot, but my main thought, or perhaps a better word is feeling, is one of complete disbelief. Surely, I say to myself, my parents must have made a mistake on my birth certificate – it is just not possible that I shall be a hundred in 12 short years (and, boy, how short the years are lately, about as long as a month was during schooldays). But truth prevails; I was born in 1916, so it's simple arithmetic.

Having accepted this, my next frequent thought is what important things do I still have to do before I quit this mortal coil, or, as slang would term it, 'pop my clogs'? It is this thinking that makes me very angry. I realise that when one is young one feels there is all the time in the world to do everything you ever want to do (including, of course, changing the world for the better!). When that annoying fact has sunk in, I find myself making lists of what I still have to do, and then having to prioritise them. This tells me that, even if I manage to live a very long life, there are many things I won't have time for this time around. I say 'this time around' because I have, after wondering about what happens after death for most of my life, come to believe in reincarnation as being the one thing which makes sense to my logical and finite brain.

My thinking has led to some action in preparing for my death from the point of view of my two sons, who will probably be left behind. I have therefore:

(a) sorted as much of my belongings as possible and marked paper stuff that can be destroyed as only of interest to me;
(b) given them complete power of attorney in case I become unable to deal with my affairs, so that they can do whatever is needed;
(c) left a list of presents I have already bought to give to people (I buy throughout the year), so that, as inevitably I may die before some are given, they can pass them on;
(d) told them when I have booked tickets for the theatre, etc. in advance, where I have put them, as it is possible I may die before the show date and they can then take someone else, with my best wishes!

As to my actual death, I must admit that the extremely un-logical part of my mind simply cannot conceive of a world which doesn't contain Jean Buzan. How on earth will they manage without me?! The practical part, however, knows that I am going to die, relatively speaking, fairly soon. So this brings me to the third question – do I worry about it? Well, in a way I suppose the answer is affirmative, but it is also partly negative. I truly am not afraid of being dead; for instance, I don't believe in purgatory or hell. But I definitely am scared of staying alive in a condition that prevents me from looking after myself – quality of life is far more important to me than quantity. So my fear is really of taking a long, helpless and especially painful time actually to die.

I most certainly do discuss all these things with other people, sometimes friends and also, surprisingly, with mere acquaintances. As a gerontologist who for many years has taught and worked with older people, I am pretty sure that the majority of 'end-of-lifers' are cognisant of this condition, and do think and talk about it.

As I am currently volunteering at a day centre for physically handicapped older people, I have managed to talk with several on this subject, both individually and as a group, and there is certainly no embarrassment or upset in broaching the subject. For some, thinking about death has been an important step in reaching a decision about their lives.

For instance, a 93-year-old lady I know once confided with me that she had a big decision to make. She had been suffering from pain for some time and had finally been told that she needed surgery to eliminate it. However, she told me that the anaesthetist had said to her, in no uncertain terms, that her heart was so weak it would most likely not survive surgery. Therefore, she explained to me, she had to make a choice: would she have the surgery and risk very likely dying, or decide against it and live longer, but with the pain? As she shared this with me she was quite calm, as if discussing which of two places to choose to go on holiday. She went on to say that she was really quite inclined towards having the surgery: 'I've had a good long life, and enjoyed it, and I really don't feel like living longer in this pain,' she said. I told her that I think, in her position, I would feel likewise.

A 70-year old woman – who, despite suffering with terrible arthritis in her hands and feet, is always bright and cheerful – had a similar decision to make: 'I have refused the offers of having replacement joints for knees, ankles, elbows, etc. as I would prefer a shorter, better-quality life than a longer one more full of operations and so on. I am absolutely determined to continue doing everything that I can for myself for as long as I possibly can. When people express surprise at how cheerful I am I just tell them, 'Well, what is the good of worrying about everything? It doesn't help make it better. You just have to do the best you can with what you have and make the most of it. It doesn't worry me that I may not have many years left because I just live from day to day, so either I have another day or I don't.'

It is interesting that when members of my group die, the attitude is always, 'Well, it was a happy release for her and we'll remember her as she was'. 'Release' is a word often used about death.

Another extremely bright lady, in her nineties, has told me she feels (and I think almost hopes) that she has had her last birthday. Because she is becoming increasingly physically frail and cannot do most of the things which used to fill her life, she feels it would be a good time to go now when she has lived a long and happy life and has so many happy memories.

In contrast, a gentleman recently turned 100 was certainly not afraid of death, nor did he dwell upon it. He actually feels he would live a lot longer and had a lot more to do, though resenting his lack of mobility and poor hearing. He just simply was unable to understand why on earth people think being 100 is so important, or means anything at all, and hated all the fuss made about it!

*Jean Buzan, 87, is a retired gerontologist living in Marlow, Buckinghamshire*

## 2    George Fullwood

The prospect of being near the end of my life is something that I have been conscious of since I was a young man. It is therefore not something that has simply emerged as a result of getting older.

In 1955 I was told I had three weeks to live. I had lived with heart disease throughout my childhood. The pain and fainting and dizziness had become a part of my everyday existence. At the age of 19 I was told I was dying.

I am now 69 years of age. I have spent major periods of my life waiting to hear whether the latest operation I have been through or treatment I have received has been successful in extending my future. I know that life may only offer me another five years but I am not dying – I am living, as I have always done. I am living a very rich and fulfilled life.

In 1967 I married a beautiful woman who I had grown up with, called Audrey. Some years later we discovered that Audrey had multiple sclerosis. We had always been strong together, and this would continue, but initially the only support we received was from each other. No one ever approached either of us to find out how we felt about living with her disease. It seemed that no one cared about what our fears were, or how we were coping, or how we could better deal with this change in our lives. Most importantly, the care we received was purely medical and supporting us in how we planned to approach the future was never considered. We just needed someone to talk with us and address the enormity of what was happening to our lives.

In April 2001 Audrey died. A huge emptiness consumed me. The love of my life had slipped away from my arms. I will never stop talking about her or remembering her. It is only when you let yourself grieve, when you are honest about how sad you feel, when life begins again. Slowly the pain eases and the gap slowly begins to fill.

It was during this time of bereavement that my experience of doctors and hospitals and indeed, the prospect of my life being at an end became the most daunting. I had spent my life in the care of doctors and nurses who at times seemed to hold my life in their hands and then, suddenly, by the sheer nature of the way doctors spoke to me and supported me, I felt scared and alone and very pressured.

I was admitted to my local Coronary Care Unit. I was a very ill man and was immediately asked if on falling unconscious I would like to be resuscitated or not. This was a question which had never been put to me in the past. Why was a doctor asking me if I wanted to be brought back to life again if I died as if he was asking if I wanted milk in my tea? Why was this something that had never been opened up as something I may have to consider in the future?

I am close to my family and I am not scared of dying but this wasn't something I wanted to talk about with them at this time. It had been put to me more pointedly than ever that this could be the end of my life. I wanted to enjoy the time I had left with my friends and family and not taint what seemed so precious with making such huge and scary decisions. I'm not saying I didn't need to talk or need someone to listen but this had to be someone independent – also someone who could allow me to make informed choices. Having choice can only be token if you don't even know what your options are.

By chance, I became friendly with a nurse who supported me in making a decision, which thankfully for me never had to be used. Fortunately since this time life has been so rich and I have enjoyed many new experiences. To think that a doctor wanted a decision made there and then as to whether or not I would choose to live if I needed to be resuscitated! To think that my life was reduced to being pressured into making such a snap decision!

I accept that I will reach the end of my life, but when I do I want to be prepared. I want to have made all the choices and decisions I need to in a measured way with the support that I need. Accepting and coping with dying is all down to being ready to move on, to leave this life behind and go to the next stage.

On reflection, being prepared for this experience would have alleviated the fear and pressure I felt at this time. Why wasn't it something that was always open for discussion with the various players in my network of care?

Everybody dies alone. It is addressing all the fears and making choices and putting your affairs in order that you need to do with other people before you go.

**George Fullwood, 69, retired engineer, Sheffield**

## 3   Dorothy Runnicles

During my adolescence and young adulthood I experienced the impact of deaths of people I knew and loved through bombing and war service activity. Only the church workers faced up to the reality of death itself and attempted to give comfort, emotional and spiritual help to those who were known to be dying and helped with the needs of those left bereaved.

Now that there are less church workers and fewer people who are helped by this route, I think we face a yawning gap – both for those who recognise that they are dying and for those experiencing the emotional and practical impacts of sharing that journey with them and the subsequent bereavement. We talk about the factors that make up the quality of life in older age. We also need to talk about the quality of dying. I am sure it is a hidden worry in many older persons' minds.

For me, with age comes more frequent contact with death and the bereaved. I think there are three important ingredients necessary for those going through the dying process. Firstly, the ingredient of Tender Loving Care [TLC] and not dying alone; secondly, the availability of effective pain killers; and thirdly, support to encourage and enable people to talk about one's own dying process, faiths and wishes and being helped to face up to the hidden fears. These fears affect people going through the process and those journeying alongside them who will be left behind, as well as those not yet clear how and when this final stage will start.

While services which provide such ingredients are out there, my experience of both the death of my mother and that of a brother within days of each other seem to suggest that the type and level of support that one receives is greatly dependent upon the circumstances in which you are dying and, in particular, whether you have been formally diagnosed as being terminally ill.

At 74, my brother was attacked by cancer which, over three months, changed him from being an active, sports-loving man into an obviously dying person. Because of his formal diagnosis of cancer, my brother's experience of the dying process was greatly enhanced by the Macmillan nurses who both assisted his wife in providing all possible TLC and the physical support, at home, from the nearby hospice where he chose to go for the last stage of his dying process. All his family members were encouraged and enabled to be with him in the hospice, including a son who was brought from another hospital to see his father. The medical and social work staff were committed to making the quality of his death as good as possible. It helped us all.

My mother's death, at 100, was different. It was a gradual but prolonged affair expressing itself in a general deterioration of her physical and mental capacities. At first, in her 70s, her full functioning was assured by my intermittent help and the help of a home help. Gradually, moving into her 80s and 90s, she needed increasing support with personal care, her finances and transport. In the last year she lost her ability to feed herself, walk and talk.

To its credit, the care home where she spent these final two years offered a daily social programme arranged by a separate worker, including outings, walks, indoor activities, discussions, bingo, pub lunches – in which she was pleased to participate. She was visited by family and friends at least two to three times per week, which also meant more outings. Her gradual mental and physical losses did not mean that she lost out on maximising what was possible.

I was called by the staff just before her hundredth birthday, when they found her unwell one morning. I asked that the doctor be called as I made my way to the home. Later in the afternoon when I arrived I could see that although my mother was not conscious she was writhing in pain. I asked for the GP to be called in again. She agreed that my mother needed painkillers for her palliative care and prescribed morphine patches for me to obtain from the chemist. It was 6.30pm. Fortunately I had a driver friend with me and we spent three and a half hours touring across London for a late-night chemist that could provide the correct prescription. My mother's obvious pain continued throughout this time, and although the sparse care staff did their best I sensed their distress and the pressure of the work.

At 10.30pm I was able to administer the patches and my mother was immediately free of pain. She died peacefully at midnight. I felt angry and disappointed at the difficulty in getting sensitive palliative arrangements for her and wondered how the staff would have managed with other deaths in the absence of any relatives' contribution.

These two experiences illustrate the enormous difference in the level and quality of emotional support from the professionals to the person dying and the family members involved. It seems that the care and support offered depends on your medical status. As a cancer patient the doors are open to services that help you through the process. However, if you are simply dying of old age there seems to be an assumption that such sensitive support is unnecessary, for you or the loved ones involved.

## What would make a difference?

The quality of hospice care should be available for all who need it. This includes those older people facing death living alone in the community and those who are living in the lonely confines of care homes. It appeared to me that the staffing level in care homes is not sufficient to ensure that older people receive the attention they need. Care assistants in residential homes and staff in hospitals need appropriate training in palliative care. GPs and community nurses need to be involved more closely with the residential care sector. Choices should be available to people known to be dying. They should be consulted on their preferences. For those journeying alongside the dying the services for bereavement counselling, for example Cruse, should be linked into those involved with older people's deaths.

.It was necessary to break down taboos relating to childbirth in my lifetime. Now we must address the other great area of non-communication. Wider discussion is needed amongst older people to remove the taboos around dying and death.

During my mother's many years in the dying process, I never felt able to discuss her wishes, awareness, faith and fears about death. Together we maximised her quality of living throughout these years but failed to provide a good quality of dying.

*Dorothy Runnicles, 79, lives in Cambridge and is an activist and advocate for the rights of older people*

## 4   Joan Rowley

I was born in England but both my parents came from Northern Ireland, and I went over there every year until the start of World War II. I was therefore introduced to religion via the Non-Subscribing Presbyterians, the most moderate and forward-looking of the Protestant churches there.

My mother died when I was four in the flu epidemic of 1918 and my father married again in 1921, his second wife being a Church of England communicant – so from then on I was introduced to their Sunday School, Brownies and Guides. As a consequence, my faith was instilled by two different church dogmas, one based on there being one God, the other on the Trinity of the Father, the Son and the Holy Ghost. I have therefore become tolerant of the teachings of different faiths, and selective in what I accept from the teachings; yet while my 'belief' in a God has remained strong, my acceptance of a particular religious teaching is not.

I still say that I am a Christian, even though I can't be a member of a specific church. If I am distressed, this is never a problem, I can still walk into a church and gain comfort from the air of peace within it. I know something beyond us will help me carry on.

As far as dying is concerned, is faith of help to older people? Of the deaths that I have witnessed faith does often seem to play an important role in making dying a peaceful process. My sister, who unlike me did have a particular faith, received help from the rector of the church. On the other hand My father also died peacefully and although he was not a member of any church his inner belief helped him.

Now I am within weeks of being 90 years old and would appreciate some discussion on how to prepare for death. I do not feel I can approach any clergyman as I do not attend church regularly and, more importantly, I am unsure whether I can ask him how I can prepare for dying when I cannot accept some concepts in the Church's teaching. Nor do I, at my time in life, wish to be 'fobbed off' with scripture readings.

In any case, what is the Church's thinking on how one should prepare for death? And why do I feel it would be embarrassing to ask for its view on this question? Is it because these questions are never asked and therefore never faced, or because they do not know how to answer it? It seems to me that, on the whole, church professionals teach us how to live, but do not fundamentally prepare us for dying.

The same seems to be true of health and social services professionals, upon whom we are likely to depend in later life to do their best to keep us alive. My stepmother died of an angina attack shortly after being discharged from hospital. She was afraid of dying and admitted it; she did not feel as safe out of the hospital. Where was the spiritual help to ease her fears? Neither the Church nor the hospital had prepared her. Again, they seem afraid to talk about death and dying.

I do not feel that I can discuss my worries with health professionals. I cannot think I am much different from the others in that I have wondered how much longer I shall be here. It is seen as morbid to talk about dying. My doctor plainly found it difficult when I said I wanted it made clear in my notes that at my age I did not want invasive surgery to take place should I not be able to make that decision for myself, and that I had already told my family this. Why the apparent embarrassment? Doctors are used to death, and if they can talk to relatives about organ donation with sensitivity, why cannot we discuss dying with them and what we would like to happen to us, or not?

Similarly, at the Primary Care Trust Strategy Board of which I am a member, the whole emphasis is on providing for the living, which is absolutely right, but we never talk about those who are dying and how they can be helped. Should I ask how they administer the morgues in the hospitals? How they prepare people who are dying to face the fact? Do they have staff trained in this 'discipline', or should they, and what the cost would be (and also would it be 'best value')?

In fact, probably the only society which talks about death in any depth is the Voluntary Euthanasia Society – a sobering thought. My understanding, however, is that those who argue for euthanasia concentrate on the fear of old age, pain and decrepitude and, it seems to me, the loss of their 'self'. I believe in the right of choice to be able to say to people who care for me that I prefer death and so do not want intervention to keep me alive. Voluntary euthanasia, however, is different: for me, it is not appropriate. I would not be able to deal with the transfer of guilt to others. I would have made the choice to die, but they might wonder why I made that choice when they could still help me. Moreover, I do not believe at present that I could go through the process and planning of euthanasia. There is a sort of horror about the actual process of killing oneself or getting someone else to kill you. I do not want to determine the date or way of death. My philosophy of life is that things die in their own good time, that one has a span of time and while unforeseen circumstances can take you away, this is not your decision. Perhaps this feeling is linked to my belief.

Coming back to myself, I have found myself shredding old files, extraneous and committee papers and then realised that I was probably 'clearing the decks'. One day I realised I was regularly reading the 'Obit' page in the *Guardian* paper, and that I was particularly noticing how many people older than me had died. I'm glad I saw the funny side of it, because I now seem to be one of a gradually diminishing circle. I wonder whether or not we do subconsciously prepare for death in this way.

I am fortunate that I have been able to talk to my daughter about my funeral, and to the clergyman of the church where my ashes will lie. I finally realised I was indeed preparing for my death when I went over to Northern Ireland this year and attended the church my ancestors have worshipped at for 270 years. I asked the Reverend's permission to have my ashes scattered in that church, and before giving it he discussed it with me and what my executors would have to do. I really appreciated that, and felt an inner peace that I have prepared as far as I can and that I shall rest finally where I want to be. Perhaps the fact that I have asked a priest in the Church of England to take my funeral service, and that I shall finally rest in a Northern Ireland Protestant church underlies my submission that I do not have a Faith, but that I do have a Belief.

*Joan Rowley, 89, is a Life Member of the Open University Students' Association and an active campaigner for the rights of older people*

## 5   Nan Maitland

In the early '80s, as the Community Care Manager for the London Borough of Bexley, I visited a large number of old people nearing the end of their lives. What I saw then was ancient, deteriorating bodies, and people who seemed to take no pleasure in life, but were just waiting to die. I did not want that for myself. I started to look for ways to escape such a grisly fate. As I became old, the possibility of these horrors drew nearer, and I started searching for information about more comfortable ways to die.

There were two powerful influences on me.

At one meeting I attended, a very old lady told us a gruesome story. She had a group of friends who arranged a tea party whenever one of them wished to die. The one to die had saved up her sleeping pills for such an occasion. She took the pills and when she became unconscious one of her friends put a plastic bag over her head; they had specially decorated her bag. Sadly, what those ladies did was legally murder, and up until that time I had no idea that, unless you had a doctor's help, there seems to be no alternative. Taking an overdose seems comparatively easy to me but the plastic bag is not something I could ask anyone else to do or do myself. The issue is not moral but emotional – a compound of fear and revulsion. I knew as I listened that this could never be an option for me. I am not interested in sanctioning such acts of murder – but I am interested in the idea of doctor-assisted suicide, whereby a doctor or nurse provides a prescription or medication in fatal dose to someone nearing the end of their life who wishes to die.

Later, at a seminar organised by the Voluntary Euthanasia Society (VES), I heard a doctor from the Northern Territories in Australia speak about people who came to him for help to die. I recognised in myself the same motivation behind the reasons those people had given to him. They were people who had always been in control of their lives and wanted to be in control of their deaths. Pain was not the key issue; it was autonomy. That was what I wanted.

Little did I know how difficult this would be.

There is a common belief amongst many older people that 'my doctor will see that I do not suffer'. Many people do not understand that there are clear legal limits to what their doctor could do, and the doctor's ability to use their discretion at the end of life is not what it used to be – for most people the only option is an increasing dose of diamorphine, which may eventually lead to death. And depending on the courage of your particular doctor and the strength of your constitution, this may mean you lie in bed doped, incontinent and without dignity, at the mercy of others for possibly many weeks, having suffered a great deal before diamorphine can even be considered. A hospice may offer a more sophisticated drug regime and better staff, but too often the same helplessness and indignity has to be endured – and often pain as well.  Not only do you suffer, but your family have to suffer while watching your long-drawn-out demise. What is the point of that?

There has been a great deal in the press and on television about an organisation called Dignitas. This organisation enables people who wish to die in comfort [to do so] with the aid of a doctor. It is based in Switzerland because, in that country, assisted suicide is decriminalised. Unless the law in the UK is changed to allow doctor-assisted suicide here, the only way to die in comfort at a time of the patient's choosing is to join Dignitas and go to Switzerland. This is what I shall do.

From this point, I have been running into a succession of obstacles. For example, if I am incapacitated and unable to take myself to Switzerland or even write a cheque, anyone helping me is liable to prosecution. I asked my solicitor whether he would release funds for an air ambulance should the need arise, and if he had a financial power of attorney. He said this would put him in a difficult position because it might be against the law.

One thing I am absolutely determined about and that is not to involve my children in my death. The guilt that they would inevitably feel if they had anything to do with the process is to be avoided at all costs. They know what I intend to do and they respect my wishes.

The reality of old age and decrepitude is something few people think about. I believe this is because our legislators and others who influence policies are not near enough to death to have started to think about what old age and death involve. Understandably they are concerned that old people should not be killed off by grasping relatives. However, doctor-assisted suicide and/or voluntary euthanasia has been legalised in The Netherlands, Belgium and the state of Oregon in the USA for some years [as well as] Switzerland. In Britain, polls have suggested that as many as 80 per cent of people favour some change in our law in this area.

I have been interested in ageing for many years and I have known many old people for whom life is a misery and they pray to God 'to take me'. I am certainly not going to wait around for God. I have arthritis now and many relatives with dementia, so that means that I have a good chance of getting dementia and my arthritis will certainly get worse. I also have a strong constitution, no heart problems, low blood pressure, low cholesterol (none of the killer diseases) and healthy, long-lived parents; so the actuarial tables say I am likely to live till 103. I am determined that I am not going to end up demented and with every movement agony, dragging on for year after miserable year till 103. Let us look clearly at what is in store for us. For some it comes early, for some later, but most of us face decreasing powers and increasing pain. The lucky ones have a killer heart attack. I have had a good life and at 78 it is still good, possibly the best time of my life, but gradually or possibly suddenly it will not be good. Life will no longer be fun, and at that point I want to be in control and say, 'Enough is enough. Goodbye.' The law must be changed so that those who wish to can end their lives when *they* want to do so in comfort.

*Nan Maitland, 78, is a retired community care manager living in London*

## 6   Shu Pao Lim

Gaining insight into older Chinese people's feelings on their own death or plans for the end of their lives is not something I have been able to do, so all I talk from is my own personal perspective and experiences.

In the Chinese community funeral ceremonies and burials are conducted in various ways depending on whether people follow Christianity, Buddhism or Taoism. Though the procedures for celebrating someone's life after death vary between faiths within the Chinese community, across all faiths there is a shared belief and attitude that talking about your own or someone else's death before the event has happened brings very bad luck and carries a bad omen.

Even from a young age, death was not something unusual or alien to me: my father was a well respected elder within our community in Burma and was often approached to help plan funerals or advise on how ceremonies should be conducted.

My father's involvement came only after the person had died. Death for Chinese people is something that is dealt with after it has happened. Any planning for their care or end of life is done at the time of it being needed by their families and friends.

I have also witnessed the death of my mother and father, sister, brother-in-law, close friends, and my own son. I have taken on the responsibility of planning and arranging their care at the end of their lives and also their funerals (be they arranged by funeral parlours, as with my own son, or crematoriums, as with my sister, or buried at the top of a mountain, as with my father).

I think it is my close and recurrent experience of death and tragedy which shaped my thinking on this matter. I have concluded that death is not something we have control over or that we can necessarily divert. When my parents were dying I realised there was nothing I could do to change the situation, and so continued with life and taking on the responsibilities that the death of both my parents left me with.

This is the same attitude I now take to my own death. While we are alive we ought to lead a healthy and meaningful life, to do the things that we like, so that when we die we will feel fulfilled and satisfied. There is nothing we can do to prevent our death. It happens to us all, and focusing on the fear or worries surrounding it cannot make it an easier experience. The only fear I have ever had of death was of someone else's and not of my own. Even then this was not a fear of dying itself but anticipation of a lingering death due to disabilities or dementia. Death is perhaps something we should embrace as it will never be avoidable. This is one of the reasons why I have prepared a living will.

My experience of planning care and funeral arrangements for others has made me more able to talk freely of my own death with my children in order that they are not burdened with such arrangements. They know where I want to live if I become more dependent and the type of funeral I would like to have.

Furthermore, for me death is not something that is final. It is simply another stage in a very long journey. We cannot possibly have learnt or experienced all we are going to in this vast world in one life. Moving on from this, the way we live our lives now can only prepare us for the next stage in our journey.

I have always known that I must approach the end of my life without worry or regret. I have prepared myself for this by trying to give as much as I can to my family and community in return for the kindness and dedication others have shown me throughout my life.

My early life in Burma and relocation to the UK carried with it much hardship and tragedy, but my strength and determination got me to where I am now, at peace. This would never be possible without the love and support of the people in my life I call my guardian angels, who gave unconditionally and whose devotion carried me through the poverty and the pain.

Very importantly, I have also learnt that having forgiveness makes for contentment. For those who stood in my way and treated me so cruelly I have only forgiveness.

It is with that security I will leave this life. I am happy that I will go without any hurt or pain in my heart, ready to receive what is waiting for me at the next stage. Somehow I know I'll be back but how or where I do not know.

*Shu Pao Lim, MBE, 81, is chair of the Camden Chinese Community Centre and the Great Wall Society*

## 7   Margaret Simey

What's it like to be 97 and in the last phase of life? After a lot of cogitating – cogitating is a very suitable occupation of the ageing –  I have come to the conclusion that I simply don't know. I can only reply, as I have done on every birthday since time began, that I feel no different. I'm still the same *me* that I have always been, the same *me* that I was yesterday and will be tomorrow.

Nevertheless, I have to accept that decrepitude creeps relentlessly on. I cannot, like King Canute when the incoming tide lapped about his ankles, gird my skirts about me and make a run for it. I may feel that I am the same *me*, but the circumstances of my life have changed and show every likelihood of changing even more every day I live.

What does it feel like to find myself in these circumstances? I have become acutely aware of the fact that my life has disintegrated into two distinct parts. There is the one that I have always regarded as the real me, the outgoing sociable person with a wide range of interests and contacts. The other is the part of my life that is responsible for the management of my daily personal affairs. I flippantly dub this other woman the 'Old Cow' in an attempt to lighten the load. All my life I have struggled to strike a balance between the two. As a woman, a mother, this feminine dilemma has been the pattern of my whole life.

Recently however I have realised that I can no longer manage this juggling act. The one I call the Old Cow has with the onward creep of physical decrepitude become more and more demanding, her needs more varied – so much so that she almost takes on an existence of her own.

This rather vague grasp of my situation was abruptly brought home to me when, a couple of years ago, I tripped over a faulty pavement and had to have a hip replacement. Since then, one mishap after another has so reduced me that I am now virtually housebound. How are the mighty fallen – quite literally!

I used to be on the side of the providers of social care, I knew my way around, what to do and who to see. I could suggest to those in need how they could tackle their particular predicaments. What a transformation! All my life committed to building up social services – now I must call on them. But now I no longer have the information, advice and reports that were available to me previously. Without that grasp of what is going on in the changing world of social care I am maddeningly frustrated.

Various assessors now arrive to determine my needs. One and all have worked through their list of tick-boxes. They decided that I did not qualify for care: all I ended up with was a commode that I didn't need. When I enquired who would empty it, the universal reply was 'we don't do that'.

Exasperated, I decided to play them at their own game by drawing up a tick-box of the list of what I expected from them:

1. Take, for example, my need for help getting in and out of my old-fashioned bath, once a week as a minimum. Answer: there is a two-year waiting list for bath attendants owing to cuts in the social services budget. No tick in that box.
2. As an alternative, social services kindly arranged for me to go instead by ambulance to a nearby day centre for a weekly bath. That worked quite well till a sharp-eyed bureaucrat intervened to say that I was just making use of the centre for baths when it was intended for full-time day care. End of baths for me. No tick in that box.
3. I asked for help in trying to find some private aid to assist with bathing. They sent a short list of care agencies but not coherent guidance: 'We don't do that'. I felt like asking them, 'What *do* you do?'. But that seemed needlessly rude.

4. The next box relates to my problem of being hard of hearing. After needless arguing I have succeeded in getting two digital hearing aids, one for each ear. These are a bit tricky to fit but the hearing aid centre insists that they cannot afford to organise a home visit to help me ('We don't do that'). Why do I have to go to their citadel like a beggar for help? I tot up the costs, in terms of hard cash, of getting me to hospital for what will possibly be a 10-minute interview, to say nothing of the indirect costs to me of tussling to get transport organised and the physical after-effects of the long day of waiting, and they are surely more costly than a home visit.
5. And finally, a source of constant frustration to me, the lack of co-ordination on the part of those who provide the services. They are rigidly organised on a demarcation basis, according to which [primary care] trust and which specialism. I am sick of being handed round like a parcel from specialism to specialism. What it boils down to is that I am the sole co-ordinator of all that is provided: a heavy burden for an old woman and one unable to hear. The choice is yours, they assure me, but I'm too old and far too ill-informed to carry such a burden.

So the essence of all this is the appalling feeling of isolation and the terrible sense of insecurity that it all brings, [together with] the expectation on me to keep up appearances, of responding brightly that I feel fine when actually I feel lousy. I tire of the struggle to keep up an interest in all that goes on about me when I am offered no place in the society in which to live my life, no part to play, no justification for my continued existence, and in the cold economic climate in which we live, no value.

I can't stand the crushing boredom of the life I now lead, busy though it keeps me. When all the days are the same, it is no wonder that I can't remember what day of the week it is, let alone what month. I weary of being grateful for the gift of a bunch of bananas or a custard tart when I am starving for something to think about. I live on the brink of not being able to manage and life is one excruciating balancing act between being able to manage and the hideous lack of trust in welfare. And if I fall over the brink and can no longer manage, is there anybody there to rescue me? The answer, I suspect, will be 'We don't do that'.

*Margaret Simey, 97, died in 2004. Having served an apprenticeship under Eleanor Rathbone, she became a life-long campaigner for social justice, focusing in later life on the rights of older people. She was a councillor in Toxteth for 23 years and a prolific writer.*

# Appendix B: National Service Framework for Older People. Standard 2: Person-centred care

9.9 Supportive and palliative care aims to promote both physical and psychosocial well-being. All those providing health and social care who have contact with older people with chronic conditions or who are approaching the end of their lives may need to provide supportive and palliative care. This may include:

**Dignity in end-of-life care**

**Information and communication**
To facilitate choice about treatments and care options for older people and their carers.

**Control of painful and other distressing symptoms**
To anticipate, recognise and treat pain and distressing symptoms, and provide timely access to appropriate specialist teams, equipment or aids. There is evidence that older people are less likely to receive proper pain management.

**Rehabilitation and support as health declines**
To ensure that quality of life and independence is maximised, and that an older person can remain at home (if that is their wish) until death or for as long as possible, through providing therapy and personal care and housing-related support services.

**Social care**
To maintain access to safe and accessible living environments, practical help, income maintenance, social networks and information.

**Spiritual care**
To recognise and meet spiritual and emotional needs through the availability of pastoral or spiritual carers reflecting the faiths of the local population.

**Complementary therapies**
To provide evidence-based complementary therapies that support emotional, psychological and spiritual well-being and help with symptom control.

**Psychological care**
To anticipate, recognise and treat any psychological distress experienced by the older person, carer or their family.

**Bereavement support**
To ensure the needs of family, friends and carers are provided for, relieving distress, meeting spiritual needs and offering bereavement counselling.

*Source: DH (2001)*

# Appendix C: Key policy landmarks in palliative and supportive care

**1980**     Report of the Working Group on Terminal Care (1980) (the Wilkes' report) produced by the Standing Subcommittee on Cancer of the Standing Medical Advisory Committee, encouraging the dissemination of the principles of terminal care throughout all sectors of the health service.

**1987**     The publication of the government's first official circular on terminal care (DH, 1987), requiring health authorities to take the lead in coordinating integrated services for terminally ill people. Palliative medicine recognised as a specialty,

**1991**     National Council for Hospice and Specialist Palliative Care established as a pressure group and begins to publish a series of influential reports and commentaries that help shape national policy.

**1992**     Standing Medical Advisory Committee and Standing Nursing and Midwifery Committee publish their report (SMAC/SNMAC, 1992) on the principles and provision of palliative care, recommending that greater effort be directed at meeting the needs of people with palliative care needs arising from non-cancer disease and in non-specialised settings.

**1995**     The Expert Advisory Group on Cancer (1995), established in 1994, reports its findings, in what is known as the Calman-Hine report. It recommends sweeping changes in the organisation of cancer and palliative care services.

**1997-2001**  New Labour Government is elected and re-elected. The NHS is reorganised, with an emphasis on national standards and strategies of care.

**1998**     The New Opportunities Fund is set up to distribute lottery money: it distributes £84 million in England in 2002-04 in grants to improve palliative care. A criterion of application is that projects encompass people with diseases other than cancer.

**2000**     ■ The NHS Cancer Plan is published, incorporating a supportive care strategy that embraces palliative care and has a key goal of providing palliative care to all those in need. Cancer and supportive/palliative care networks established.
■ The National Council for Hospice and Specialist Palliative Care Services sends out for consultation proposals for a National Plan and Strategic Framework for Palliative Care 2000-05.
■ The 2000 Care Standards Act leads to the establishment of the Care Standards Commission, which has the remit of inspecting palliative care provision within care homes and voluntary sector hospices[1].

---

[1] At the time of writing, the Care Standards Commission was replaced by two bodies: the Commission for Health Audit and Inspection (CHAI) to cover hospices, and the Commission for Social Care Inspection to cover care homes.

| 2001 | The National Service Framework for Older People is published (DH, 2001) and makes explicit reference to the value of palliative care for older people. |
| --- | --- |
| **2003** | The government announces the release of £12 million to improve the care of the dying (www.info.doh.gov.uk/dog/intpress.nsf/page/2003-0530). |
| **2004** | National Institute for Clinical Excellence publishes its guidance on cancer services, entitled *Improving supportive and palliative care for adults with cancer* (NICE, 2004). |

*Source:* Adapted from Davies and Seymour (2002)

# Appendix D: National minimum standards. Standard 11: Dying and death

Outcome: Service users are assured that at the time of their death, staff will treat them and their family with care, sensitivity and respect.

**Standard 11**

| | |
|---|---|
| 11.1 | Care and comfort are given to service users who are dying, their death is handled with dignity and propriety, and their spiritual needs, rites and functions observed. |
| 11.2 | Care staff make every effort to ensure that the service user receives appropriate attention and pain relief. |
| 11.3 | The service user's wishes concerning terminal care and arrangements after death are discussed and carried out. |
| 11.4 | The service user's family and friends are involved (if that is what the service user wants) in planning for and dealing with increasing infirmity, terminal illness and death. |
| 11.5 | The privacy and dignity of the service user who is dying are maintained at all times. |
| 11.6 | Service users are able to spend their final days in their own rooms, surrounded by their personal belongings, unless there are strong medical reasons to prevent this. |
| 11.7 | The registered person ensures that staff and service users who wish to offer comfort to a service user who is dying are enabled and supported to do so. |
| 11.8 | Palliative care, practical assistance and advice, and bereavement counselling are provided by trained professionals/specialist agencies if the service user wishes. |
| 11.9 | The changing needs of service users with deteriorating conditions or dementia for personal support or technical aids are reviewed and met swiftly to ensure the individual retains maximum control. |
| 11.10 | Relatives and friends of a service user who is dying are able to stay with him/her, unless the service user makes it clear that he or she does not want them to, for as long as they wish. |
| 11.11 | The body of a service user who has died is handled with dignity, and time is allowed for family and friends to pay their respects. |
| 11.12 | Policies and procedures for handling dying and death are in place and observed by staff. |

(DH, 2002, pp 13-14)

# Appendix E: Principles of a good death

To know when death is coming, and to understand what can be expected.

To be able to retain control of what happens.

To be afforded dignity and privacy.

To have control over pain relief and other symptom control.

To have choice and control over where death occurs (at home or elsewhere).

To have access to information and expertise of whatever kind is necessary.

To have access to any spiritual or emotional support desired.

To have access to hospice care in any location, not only in hospital.

To have control over who else is present and shares the end.

To be able to issue advance directives which ensure wishes are respected.

To have time to say goodbye, and control over other aspects of timing.

To be able to leave when it is time to go, and not to have life prolonged pointlessly.

(Debate of the Age Health and Care Study Group, 1999, p 42)

# Depression and older people
## Towards securing well-being in later life

**Mary Godfrey** with **Tracy Denby**, Institute of Health Sciences and Public Health Research, University of Leeds

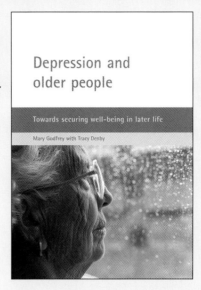

*"We know too little about depression in later life. It hasn't been taken seriously enough. Here is a report that sets out the issues clearly and makes recommendations that are realisable."* **Heather Clark, School of Social Studies, University College Chichester**

The literature on depression in old age has tended to be dominated by the medical model with its focus on symptoms and treatment. This report breaks new ground by adopting a psycho-social approach - one that explores depression in the context of the everyday lives of older people.

Commissioned by Help the Aged, the report:

*   reviews the nature and scope of the evidence base around depression and older people;
*   evaluates current policy and practice responses;
*   identifies gaps in the evidence base and areas for further work.

Depression and older people is invaluable reading for anyone involved in the management and delivery of services to older people, as well as academics, students and researchers in the field. It will also be of interest to older people themselves.

**Contents**: Introduction; Later life with depression: nature and prevalence; The experience of depression; Risk and vulnerability; Accessing help from primary and community care; Models of treatment and care in later life depression; Securing well-being in older age; Summary and conclusions.

A4 REPORT £14.99 US$25.00 ISBN 1 86134 642 5
297 x 210mm 64 pages November 2004
Published in association with Help the Aged

To order, please contact:

**In the UK and Europe:**
Marston Book Services, PO Box 269, Abingdon, Oxon, OX14 4YN, UK
Tel: +44 (0)1235 465500, Fax: +44 (0)1235 465556
Email: direct.orders@marston.co.uk

**In the USA and Canada:**
ISBS, 920 NE 58th Street, Suite 300, Portland, OR 97213-3786, USA
Tel: +1 800 944 6190 (toll free), Fax: +1 503 280 8832
Email: info@isbs.com

**In Australia and New Zealand:**
DA Information Services, 648 Whitehorse Road Mitcham, Victoria 3132, Australia
Tel: +61 (3) 9210 7777, Fax: +61 (3) 9210 7788
E-mail: service@dadirect.com.au

For further information about these and other titles published by The Policy Press, please visit our website at:
www.policypress.org.uk

Help the Aged